MAINE
FISHING MAPS
◆
VOLUME 2 - RIVERS AND STREAMS

Text by
Harry Vanderweide

Maps by
DeLorme Mapping Company

ISBN 0-89933-038-X
©1991 DeLorme Mapping
Freeport, Maine 04032
All rights reserved.

INDEX

INTRODUCTION

A book about fishing rivers in Maine necessarily covers a lot of territory. The reason is that the word "river" is not a precise term, but includes everything from raging torrents to gentle trickles. For the purpose of this book, river simply means water which flows, without regard to amount.

Included here are waters as diverse as imaginable, because that is the nature of rivers. There is little similarity between the gentle undulations of Belgrade Stream as it flows from Long Pond to Messalonskee Lake and the brawling West Branch of the Penobscot as it roars from its gorge at Ripogenus Dam and then through a series of the most impressive falls in Maine.

Even various stretches of a single river can offer such sharp contrasts. The Sheepscot River above Route 105 is a large brook with populations of brook and brown trout and landlocked salmon which feed on mayflies, while below the Route 1 bridge in Wiscasset it is a broad salt water estuary where flounder, mackerel and stripers chase sand eels and marine worms.

We have assumed that the fascination is with water which flows and have made no attempt to refine our coverage any further. We have included rivers of all sorts here; thus a six foot fly rod that casts a four weight fly line may be appropriate for some of these rivers, while a solid trolling rod and lead core line may suit another.

There is a fact of rivers the reader should keep in mind as he refers to the information in this volume. Rivers are not constant, but change from moment to moment. In comparison to a river, a lake is static. It has well-defined margins which are altered only slowly and the temperature and clarity of its water tend to change gradually.

But rivers change hourly, sometimes minute by minute. Even when no particularly violent weather conditions are affecting rivers they are changeable. For example, a stream may be 20 degrees warmer at noon than it was at 5 a.m. Spring run-off can increase a river's volume by 100 times. Sudden summer rain can alter it from gin clear to the color of coffee with milk in an hour or two. Many of our rivers are dammed and the demands of hydro-electric generation cause flow levels to fluctuate widely. Many of our coastal rivers change their direction of flow every six hours as the tide rises and falls. All of these factors naturally affect the fishability of a given river, making them much more challenging to deal with successfully. This is no doubt the reason why lakes and ponds are so much more popular with the general angler.

While we are pointing out the changeability of our rivers, we should note that the number of fish residing in a river is also variable. Most of our upland rivers are largely fed by run-off and do not have significant fish populations throughout long periods of the year. The fish in such rivers retreat to lakes and ponds whenever the water is too high, too cold, too muddy, too warm or too low. In some cases, the good fishing in a stream may last only a couple of weeks as fish move in to take advantage of ideal temperatures and water levels for spawning or feeding on insect hatches or baitfish runs. In many of our coastal rivers, runs of anadromous fish, such as the Atlantic salmon, have definite seasons. Then there are salt water fish, such as mackerel and bluefish, which are only along our shores during the warm summer months; both will ascend far up coastal rivers.

Most readers of this book will be particularly interested in landlocked salmon and trout. These fish are present in some of our rivers year round, but in the southern two thirds of the state such waters are extremely limited. In fact, the portions of the Kennebec River below Wyman Dam and the West Branch of the Penobscot River below Ripogenus Dam are the major examples.

As a general guideline, we believe there are definite month-long seasons when the landlocked salmon and trout fishing are prime in Maine rivers and streams. It is an over-simplification, but following these seasons for various parts of the state can help you plan fishing trips for trout and landlocked salmon when the conditions will be most favorable. The first season would hold in the southern third of the state, in the area generally to the south of Bangor. The best time to fish trout and salmon rivers in this area would be from the third week of May to the third week of June. The second season would be in the middle third of the state, roughly that area from Bangor to Houlton. This area would be best from the first of June to the end of the month. The third season would be in the area north of Houlton where the fishing would be best from the second week of June to the second week of July.

Naturally there are plenty of exceptions to such seasons. We have found, for example, that fishing in the Rangeley-Flagstaff area streams holds up well until the middle of July. Certainly, amounts of rain and temperatures can alter these seasons as well. We offer them only as a general guide to point out that the further north you go in this state, the later the good fishing occurs.

We would also point out that the brook trout is ubiquitous in Maine. In the northern two thirds of the state brookies probably exist in well over 90 percent of the rivers and streams. While their abundance and size may vary widely from stream to stream they can be found in the biggest rivers and the tiniest streams, including trickles which all but dry up in the summertime. As most of the streams in the southern end of the state are too warm for brook trout to survive year round, many brooks and streams in York and Cumberland counties are stocked annually.

One of the problems the author had in writing the descriptions in this book was determining how to present the material. For example, the Kennebec River is 125 miles long from its twin outlets at Moosehead Lake to the ocean at Popham Beach. It presents many different fishing opportunities along the way, from landlocked salmon at the East and West outlets, to rainbow trout below Wyman Dam, brown trout below Solon, smallmouth bass in the Skowhegan area, Atlantic salmon below the Augusta dam and striped bass at Phippsburg.

What we have done is to divide such rivers into sections based on such considerations as access, geography, fish species, dams, size and water type. You will find that this has resulted in some of the sections covered being many miles long while others cover very limited areas. In a way this makes great sense because that is also the way our rivers are fished. In some of them all of the action is centered around a limited area, such as a dam or a waterfall, while others offer good fishing over long stretches. This observation is also something which you as a fisherman want to keep in mind as you consider fishing rivers.

We have included directions on how to get to the sections of rivers covered in this volume as well as we can, but suggest that you obtain a copy of DeLorme's Maine Atlas and Gazetteer to better orient yourself in following those directions.

This book is the most comprehensive gathering of river angling information ever done on the Pine Tree State and we believe we have provided good information on most of the best waters in the state. However, since there are 37,000 miles of rivers in Maine, no single author or book could ever cover all the possibilities. In general, this book covers only the major rivers, with the basic criterion being that they are at least 20 miles long (there are exceptions such as Grand Lake Stream, an internationally known river which would have to be included in any book on Maine rivers).

Another point about this book is that it is limited to the where-to, when-to aspects of river fishing and is not a how-to book. Plenty of excellent books have been written explaining in tremendous detail how to fish the various kinds of fish found in Maine in all sorts of conditions. What no book has ever done before is to tell you how to find exactly where these fish are and when to go after them.

You will notice we've made little attempt to include current fishing regulations for any of these rivers. The reason is that regulations are determined by men and subject to abrupt change while the basic information this book provides is stable: the best times to fish, what fish are available, and what sections to fish.

River fishing in Maine offers a diversity which is unmatched by lake and pond fishing. It ranges from the urban surroundings of the Bangor Salmon Pool on the main stem of the Penobscot River, to the wilderness setting of Caucomgomoc Stream. In this book we have tried to cover both those extremes and all the wonderful river fishing opportunities in between. We hope you'll enjoy the book as much as we have writing it.

Harry Vanderweide

CREDITS

Thanks to the following for contributing information to this book: Wilmot Robinson, Bill Graves, Sherwood Chandler, David O'Connor, David DeLorme, Doug Jowett, Nate Mitchell, Roger D'Errico, Al Meister, and Bill Hubbard.

MAINE'S STOCKED RIVERS

As a general rule, the Maine Fish and Wildlife Department does not stock rivers or streams, but there are exceptions. The major exceptions are small streams in the southernmost portion of the state where summer water temperatures are too high for trout to live. Brook trout are stocked on a put and take basis to provide spring fishing. A second large segment of stream stocking is devoted to the establishment of brown trout in certain streams where it is hoped they will become self-sustaining or where they are needed to supplement the natural population.

Here are the streams which are routinely stocked, the location the fish are put in, and the species of fish stocked.

Androscoggin County

Androscoggin River, Lewiston/Brunswick, Brown Trout
Androscoggin River, Turner, Brown Trout
Nezinscot River, Turner, Brown Trout

Aroostook County

B Stream, Houlton, Brook Trout

Cumberland County

Jordan River, Raymond, Landlocked Salmon
Northwest River, Sebago, Landlocked Salmon
Pleasant River, Gray, Brook Trout
Presumpscot River, Westbrook, Brown Trout
Presumpscot River, Windham, Landlocked Salmon
Royal River, New Gloucester, Brook and Brown Trout
Royal River, Yarmouth, Brown Trout

Franklin County

Carrabasset River, North New Portland, Brook Trout
Dead River, North Branch, Chain of Ponds, Brook Trout
Dead River, South Branch, Poplin/Dallas, Brook Trout

Kennebec County

Carrabasset Stream, Clinton, Brown Trout
Kennebec River, Madison, Brown Trout
Kennebec River, Solon, Brown Trout
Kennebec River, Waterville/Sidney, Brown Trout
Messalonskee Stream, Oakland, Brown Trout

Knox County

St. George River, Appleton/Warren, Brown Trout

Lincoln County

Medomak River, Waldoboro, Brown Trout
Pemaquid River, Bremen, Brown Trout

Oxford County

Androscoggin River, Bethel, Brown Trout
Androscoggin River, Gilead/Bethel, Brook Trout
Crooked River, Albany, Landlocked Salmon
Ellis River, West Branch, Andover, Brook Trout
Nezinscot River, Buckfield, Brown Trout
Wild River, Gilead, Brook Trout

Somerset County

Indian Stream, St. Albans, Brown Trout
Sheepscot River, Somerville/Palermo, Brown Trout

Washington County

Grand Lake Stream, Grand Lake Stream, Brook Trout
Middle River, Marshfield, Brook Trout

York County

Cape Neddick River, York, Brown Trout
Great Works River, Sanford, Brook and Brown Trout
Kennebunk River, Dayton, Brown Trout
Little Ossipee River, Newfield, Brown Trout
Little River, Lebanon, Brook and Brown Trout
Merriland River, Wells, Brown Trout
Mousam River, Kennebunk, Brown Trout
Ogunquit River, Wells, Brown Trout
Saco River, Hollis/Dayton, Brown Trout

MAINE COUNTY MAP

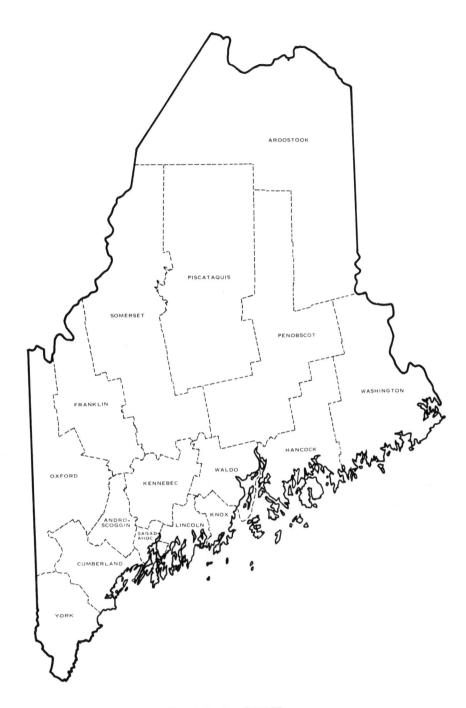

SPECIAL NOTE

This book does not include current fishing regulations which are changing constantly. Such regulations cover size and bag limits, closed sections, equipment restrictions and seasons. We suggest that anyone not intimately familiar with the regulations on a particular piece of water consult the latest issue of the Open Water Fishing Regulations. Those interested in Atlantic salmon should review the current issue of the latest Atlantic salmon regulations. Both of these publications are available by writing to the Department of Inland Fisheries and Wildlife, 284 State Street, Augusta, Maine 04333.

There are a number of other publications by DeLorme Mapping Company which can be used in conjunction with the maps in this book. The Maine Atlas and Gazeteer is probably the most useful in figuring out long distance routes between fishing areas. For specific areas there are map and guides on The Allagash and St. John, Baxter State Park, Sebago Lake and Moosehead Lake. You can order these maps and guides by writing to: DeLorme Mapping Company, P.O. Box 298, Freeport, Maine 04032.

LEGEND OF MAP SYMBOLS

═══════════	Dual lane highway
══════════	State route
──────────	Other passable roads
‑ ‑ ‑ ‑ ‑ ‑ ‑ ‑	Unimproved road
– – – – – – –	Trail
━━━━━━━━━	Major urban road
────────	Minor urban road
─ ‑‑ ─ ‑‑ ─	State boundary
─ ‑ ─ ‑ ─	County boundary
+++++++++	Railroad

⊖	Fish hatchery
♠	Park/recreation area
▭	Boat launch - hand carry
◖	Boat launch - paved
⊼	Picnic or rest area
Å	Maintained forest campsite
Λ	Primitive campsite - permit required for open fire
Ⱦ	Lookout tower
♠	Ranger station
♔	Forest gatehouse
⋈	Customs station
⊢‑×	Gate or barricade
1400	Land elevation - feet above sea level
998	Water elevation - feet above sea level
o	Bridge out/road blocked
	Best Fishing Area

NORTH ORIENTATION: North is to the top of the page on all maps unless otherwise indicated.

The maps in this book are not intended for navigational use. The information in this book does not imply any fishing regulations or landowner permission. Current fishing regulations must be observed and private property or landowner restrictions must be respected.

Abol Stream
Confluence Penobscot River, West Branch

Piscataquis County
Maine Atlas maps 50,51

The area where Abol Stream joins the West Branch is the only portion of the stream worth bothering with because the rest of it runs through steep terrain with clear mountain run-off which generally blocks trout passage.

The lower end of the stream is a huge, beaver-pond-like flowage with many channels running through it. For the most part, the best action is found close to the West Branch. Boats and canoes anchor or troll here in hopes the short length of stream which provides cold water will attract fish. Access is via the Golden Road to the Abol Bridge or by taking Route 157 to Millinocket and travelling the road to Baxter State Park.

Good fishing lasts from June to September and the wading is easy except close to the West Branch. The last half mile can be canoed. The quarry is brook trout in the 8 to 12 inch range. Don't expect to find major insect hatches here.

Scale ½″ = 1 Mile

Miles

Alder Stream
Alder Stream Township

Franklin County
Maine Atlas map 29

Besides lovely native brook trout, Alder Stream offers the angler plenty of wildlife sighting possibilities. The sandy shores of this small stream are often pocked with deer and moose tracks while grouse drum in the mixed growth on the surrounding hillsides. About the first week of June the fiddleheading is excellent.

Alder Stream is one of the most easily waded pieces of water in Maine, with a lot of sand and smooth gravel. It is ideal fly fishing water with frequent caddis and mayfly hatches. Brookies are abundant here, but a 13-incher is a good fish.

Best fishing is during June and the first two weeks of July; later if the water level holds up. Access is from Route 27 north of Eustis. Watch carefully for a dirt road (rough but usually passable by passenger cars) on the left as you drive north. If you cross the bridge you'll know you've missed it. There is a tent campground just shortly after you get onto this road.

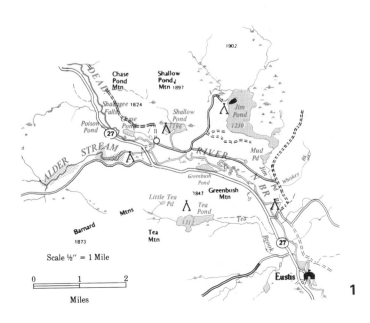

Scale ½″ = 1 Mile

0   1   2

Miles

1

Allagash River
Telos Landing to Allagash

**Piscataquis and Aroostook Counties
Maine Atlas maps 55, 56, 57, 60, 61, 62, 63, 66, 67**

The Allagash River is the focal point of a 200,000 acre wilderness waterway preserve that is one of Maine's major canoe trip attractions. Trips on the Allagash can be arranged to encompass any amount of time, but it generally takes 4 to 7 days to make the trip from Telos Lake to Allagash Village. Along the way, the canoeist crosses many lakes in addition to travelling the river.

There are lake trout and whitefish in the lakes, but the river itself contains primarily brook trout, mostly in the 8 to 10-inch range. Probably the best time to fish this river is in June when brook trout can be encountered almost anyplace. In July and August the fish will be concentrated around brook mouths and near spring holes. Brook trout fishing on the surface can also be excellent around the islands, gravel bars and inlets of Churchill and Eagle Lakes·

Anyone considering fishing the Allagash, or making a canoe trip down the river, should obtain a copy of DeLorme's Allagash and St. John Guide, which, besides being the most detailed map of the region available, also contains a wealth of information on the various trips that can be made down the waterway.

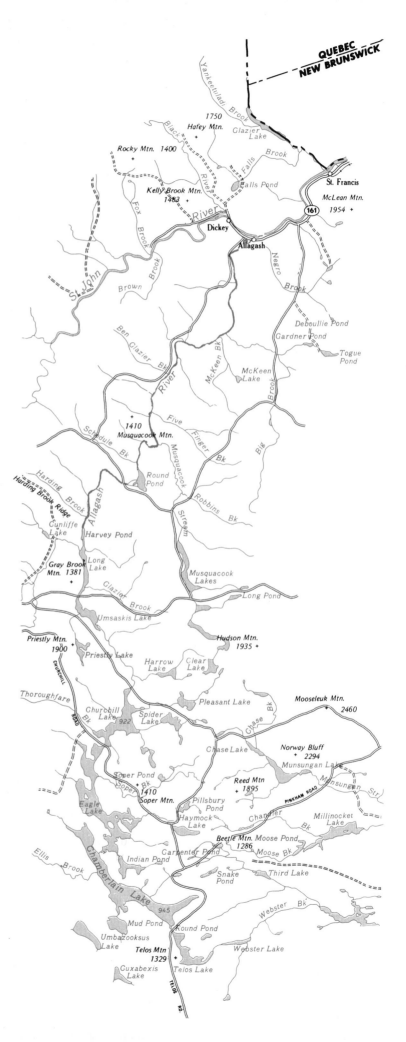

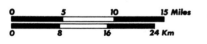

Androscoggin River
Brunswick & Topsham

Sagadahoc and Cumberland Counties
Maine Atlas map 6

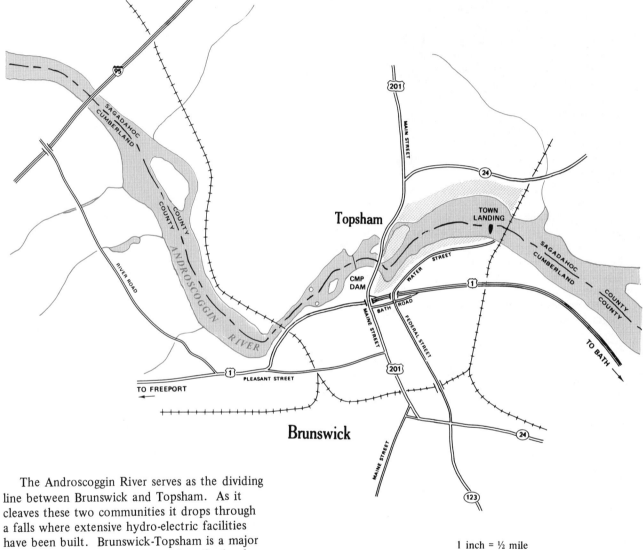

The Androscoggin River serves as the dividing line between Brunswick and Topsham. As it cleaves these two communities it drops through a falls where extensive hydro-electric facilities have been built. Brunswick-Topsham is a major commercial and tourist area and heavily developed.

It is possible to fish from shore in this section, but a boat or canoe proves much more productive. There is a rough, all-tide launching area located on the south shore below the Route 201 bridge. From Maine Street turn on to Bath Road and immediately bear left onto Water Street where the launch is located.

The river just below the dam is a hotspot for both striped bass and white perch. It also has a good run of sea-run brown trout, brook trout and an occasional Atlantic salmon gets lost and finds its way into the fast water below the Route 201 bridge. The stream that enters the

river just east of the railroad trestle is a good spot too, as it is a breeding area for sea-run brookies.

You can expect to catch stripers from mid-May through June, which also is a good time to try for white perch. The stripers are school fish which range from 2 to 5 pounds. Seaworms will take them, but gold Rapalas and Al's Goldfish are also good bets. You would be most likely to pick up brown trout up to 10 pounds during the first two weeks of June.

1 inch = ½ mile

0   ½   1 mile

3

Aroostook River
Headwaters to Ashland

Aroostook, Piscataquis and Penobscot Counties
Maine Atlas maps 57, 58, 63, 64, 65

The fishing in this section of the Aroostook is rated "very good" by the locals. The quarry is brook trout and landlocked salmon with the possibility of an Atlantic salmon added as spice. The best fishing is from late May to late June with hatches of small mayflies in June and July and some larger mayflies and caddis in July and August.

The river bottom is gravelly, interspersed with rocks, with sections which can be waded. Most years canoeing conditions are good and craft can be put in or taken out at Munsungen Stream, Millinocket Stream, Arbo Flats, Masardis, Garfield Road and the Ashland Fish and Game Club.

The Oxbow checkpoint is a fee gate. Usually the person managing it can provide information on good sections of the river to fish and the current conditions. In hot weather try the mouth of any of the numerous feeder streams. The Mooseleuk inlet is excellent. The brook trout are in the 8 to 10-inch range and the landlocked salmon range up to 5 pounds.

Access is from Route 11 and the headwaters are reached by the Oxbow Road which is controlled by North Maine Woods.

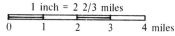

1 inch = 2 2/3 miles

0   1   2   3   4 miles

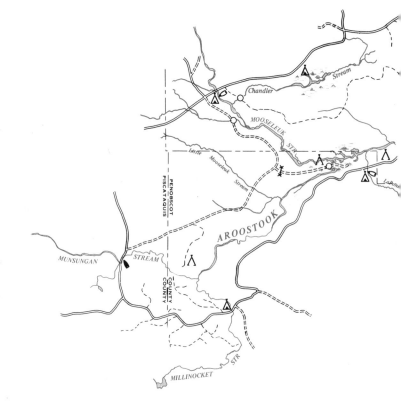

4

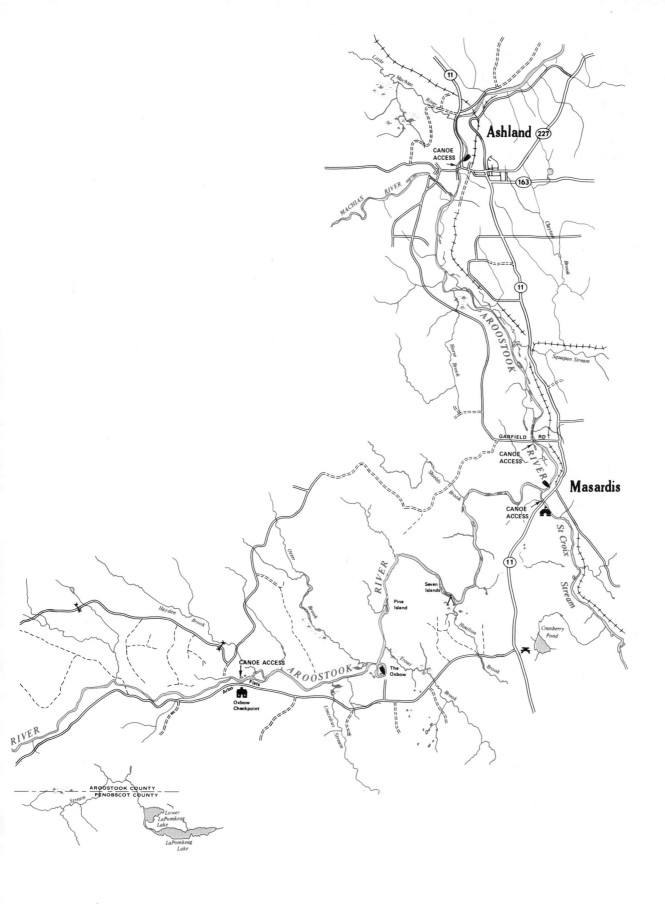

Aroostook River

Ashland to the Canadian Border

Aroostook County
Maine Atlas maps 58, 64, 65

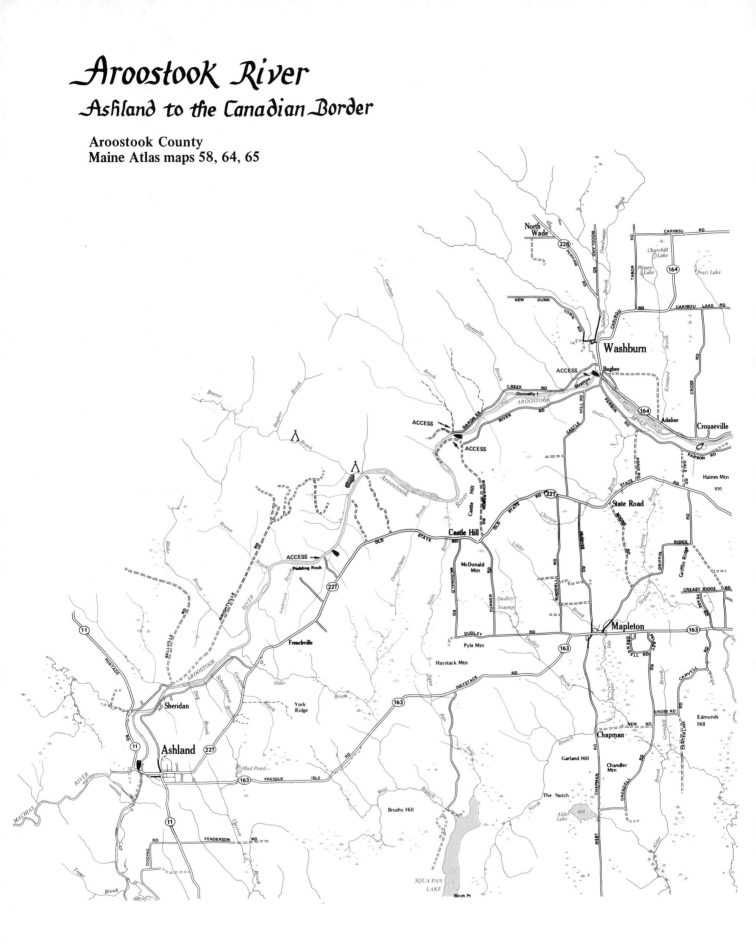

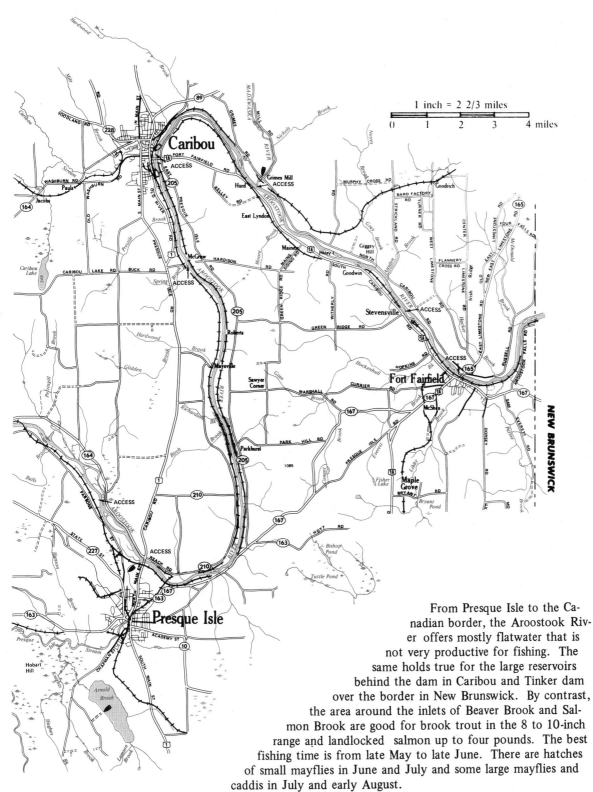

1 inch = 2 2/3 miles

0   1   2   3   4 miles

From Presque Isle to the Canadian border, the Aroostook River offers mostly flatwater that is not very productive for fishing. The same holds true for the large reservoirs behind the dam in Caribou and Tinker dam over the border in New Brunswick. By contrast, the area around the inlets of Beaver Brook and Salmon Brook are good for brook trout in the 8 to 10-inch range and landlocked salmon up to four pounds. The best fishing time is from late May to late June. There are hatches of small mayflies in June and July and some large mayflies and caddis in July and early August.

The river bottom is largely rocky interspersed with gravel sections and there are some wadeable sections. Most of the major tributaries provide places to carry in or take out a canoe as do the road bridge crossings.

From Ashland to Washburn the river is banked by a mixture of farm and wood land and from Washburn to the border it flows through urban and farming areas.

To find this section of river drive Route 1 to Presque Isle or Route 11 to Ashland.

Belgrade Stream
Long Pond to Messalonskee Lake

Kennebec County
Maine Atlas map 12

You can fish this stream from the various bridges that cross it, or even from shore, but a canoe or boat is really required to cover much water.

This is gentle flatwater that offers prime fishing for smallmouth and largemouth bass, plus white and yellow perch and the occasional pickerel. About the middle of May it is possible to make contact with a migrating brown trout or landlocked salmon. The section above the Wings Mills dam going toward Long Pond is best for smallmouth bass.

Best access is to take the Belgrade exit off I-95 and follow Route 27 north to Messalonskee Lake. Sizeable boats can be put in at the state boat launch off Route 27 in Belgrade although craft much over 14 feet are really too big to venture far upstream. Canoes can be put in at the Route 135 bridge or at the Wings Mills dam.

It is possible to troll this weedy stream, but casting is the best route to take. Fishing is good from June through September, but you'll want to fish early or late in the day during the hottest times of the year. Although much of the surrounding area is developed, much of the stream flows through gently rounded hills of mixed growth and farmland and is a very attractive area to fish.

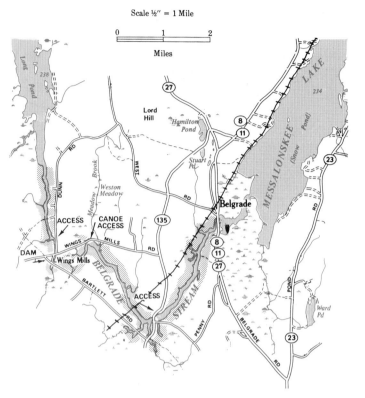

Scale ½" = 1 Mile

Carrabassett River
New Portland to North Anson

Somerset County
Maine Atlas map 20

The wire bridge located in New Portland makes the Carrabassett River unique, for nowhere else in the state is there a free suspension wire supported bridge.

A lot of people who visit the wire bridge also stop to fish the riffle area above and below the bridge. Although this is an attractive area and looks like classic fly fishing water, it isn't very productive. A canoe can be put in on the north side of the river and ridden downstream although in late summer the water may be too low. There are numerous spots along Route 16 where a canoe can be taken out.

Closer to North Anson the river becomes deeper and wider, making it more suitable for fishing from the bank or canoe than for wading. In the past there have been rainbow trout in the river although this fishery never developed much. Now brook trout are probably the river's greatest attraction.

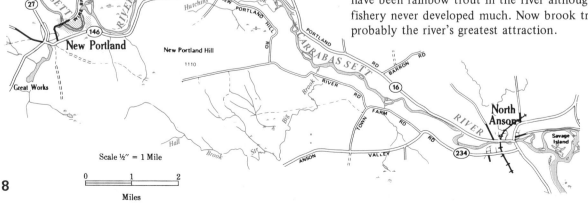

Scale ½" = 1 Mile

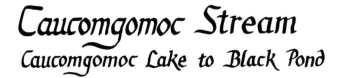

Caucomgomoc Stream
Caucomgomoc Lake to Black Pond

Piscataquis County
Maine Atlas maps 49, 55

The most direct way to get to this remote stream is by flying in to Caucomgomoc Lake. Another possibility is travelling up Chesuncook Lake by boat and then up Black Pond to get to the lower reaches of this relatively short stream. The usual approach, however, is to haul a boat in from Rockwood over the road north to the 20 Mile Check Point and then east to Seboomook Dam to the Golden Road. Take Golden Road to Ragmuff Gate and follow the woods road north to Caucomgomoc Check Point where there is a campground. You would then motor six miles across Caucomgomoc Lake to get to the dam and the stream.

Is it worth all the bother? A lot of anglers think so and they make the effort to get to the stream to fish for landlocked salmon which average two pounds, but can get up to seven or eight pounds.

This is wild, rugged country and steep banks line the stream, but there are many pools which offer easy fishing. The wading is not difficult, although conditions are slippery. Best fishing is in June and early July and there are good hatches of caddis flies, particularly a brownish yellow in size 14. If you make this trip by land instead of flying in, plan to camp and fish for several days to make it worth your while. If you cross the lake to get to the stream be careful as even in mid-summer whitecaps can whip up on Caucomgomoc Lake.

Scale ½″ = 1 Mile

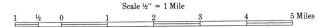

Cobbosseecontee Stream
Cobbosseecontee Lake to Kennebec River

Kennebec and Sagadahoc Counties
Maine Atlas map 12

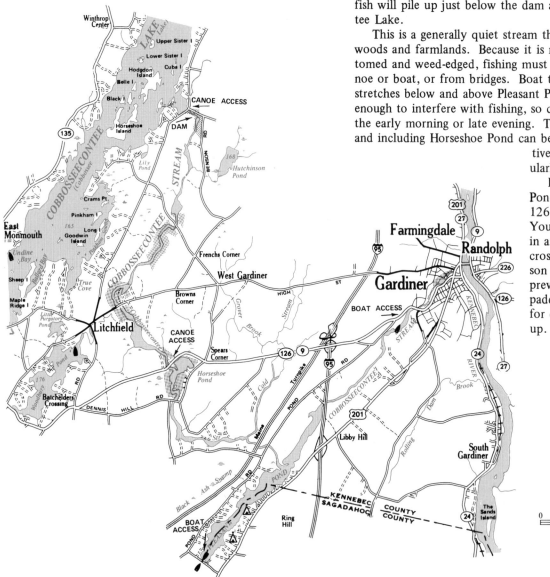

Largemouth bass in the 7 to 8 pound range are caught in Cobbossee (the truncated version of Cobbosseecontee) stream each year. The bass, pickerel and yellow perch fishing is good all through the summer, although mid-June is probably best. Often good fish will pile up just below the dam at Cobbosseecontee Lake.

This is a generally quiet stream that flows through woods and farmlands. Because it is mostly mud-bottomed and weed-edged, fishing must be done in a canoe or boat, or from bridges. Boat traffic in the stretches below and above Pleasant Pond can be heavy enough to interfere with fishing, so consider going in the early morning or late evening. The area around and including Horseshoe Pond can be very productive for bass, partiularly in September.

Follow High Street, Pond Road or Route 126 out of Gardiner. You can put a canoe in anywhere a road crosses. In early season the current may prevent upstream paddling so arrange for downstream pickup.

Scale ½″ = 1 Mile

Miles

Crooked River
Bolsters Mills to Sebago Lake

Cumberland and Oxford Counties
Maine Atlas maps 4,5,10,11

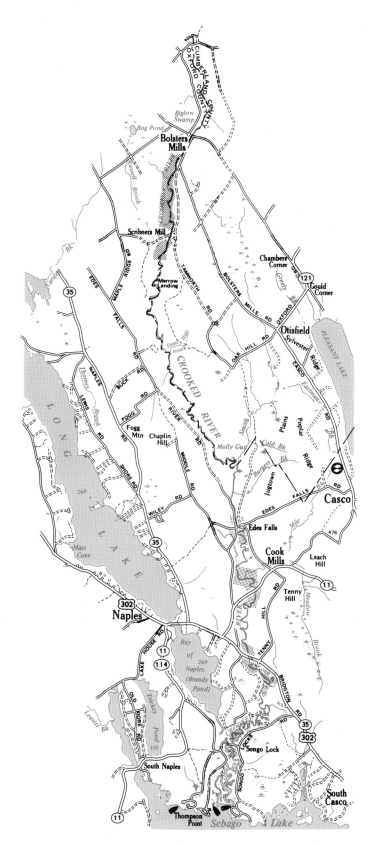

The Crooked River is southern Maine's leading landlocked salmon stream, gaining strength from being a major tributary of Sebago Lake, southern Maine's outstanding landlocked lake.

There are deadwater areas behind the dams at Edes Falls, Scribners Mill, and Bolsters Mills, but these are also some of the best fishing areas along the river. Salmon have been known to hold in the rapids and eddies below Bolsters Mills throughout the season. Walk the stream banks or wade down the river to find the best water. There are good pools both above and below the dam at Scribners Mill. There is a lot of turbulent water below Scribners which turns into good pools and gentle riffles just beyond sight of the dam. There is a logging road along the left bank that provides easy access to these stretches.

Edes Falls and the pool at Mile Brook, upstream from Route 11, are easily reached. There is a foot trail along the right hand bank leading to sections which vary from deep pools to riffles.

Early in the season you might want to try just up or downstream from Route 302, or the confluence of the Crooked and Songo Rivers near the Songo Locks. This is one of the opening day favorite places to fish and competition can be intense.

The Crooked offers a good run of fish in September, particularly after the 15th, but check the law book carefully for latest regulations. A 2-pound fish will cause few eyebrows to rise when it comes from the Crooked and salmon in the 5- to 6-lb. range can be expected. This is a good river to fish nymphs and streamer imitations. There are good hatches of caddis and mayflies emerging about mid-May through the third week of June.

The *Sebago Lake Map & Guide,* available from DeLorme Mapping Company, shows Sebago Lake and environs in full-color and high detail, with text about recreation and history of the area.

Scale ½" = 1 Mile

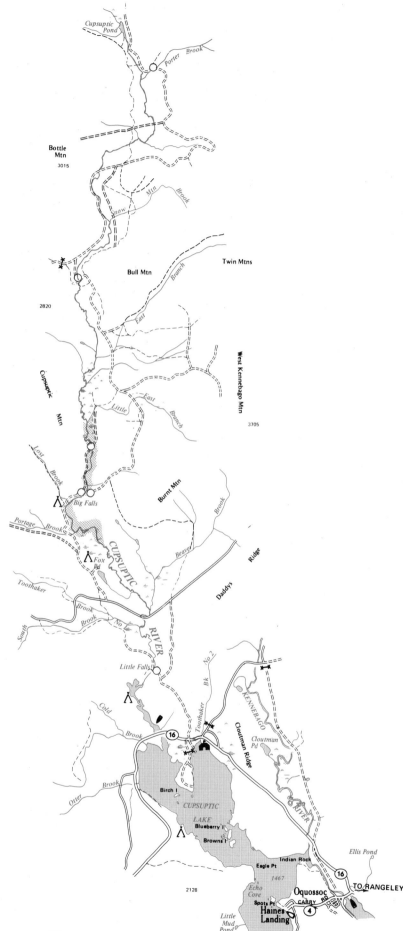

Cupsuptic River
Cupsuptic Pond
to Cupsuptic Lake

Oxford County
Maine Atlas map 28

The Cupsuptic River flows rapidly down-hill from remote Cupsuptic Pond near the Canadian Border, but it does have a good population of brook trout in the 8 to 10-inch range. Finding the river is not easy: from Rangeley take Route 16 west, pass the Maine Forest Service station on the left and take the next dirt road to the right. The dirt roads can be rough to travel.

The brook trout in this stream seem fond of nymphs in dark colors in sizes 8 to 12. A dark Cahill wet fly is also a good bet.

The stream flows through rugged country with alternating rapids and pools. The area around Big Falls is productive in the month of June.

Scale ½″ = 1 Mile

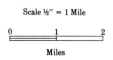

Miles

Damariscotta River
Damariscotta to Atlantic Ocean

Lincoln County
Maine Atlas map 7

The Damariscotta River below the town of Damariscotta is a classic example of a long coastal estuary: so well protected from wind and ocean waves that it can be safely traversed by small boats in all but the worst weather.

There is an excellent boat launch right in the downtown area, just behind the stores after you cross over the Route 1B bridge. Boats can be launched at all tides.

Stripers up to 50 pounds have been caught just below the bridge where impressive eddies form on the outgoing tide. Try fishing this spot after dark, using live eels in the backwaters that form as the tide rushes out below the bridge.

Mackerel are also found in the river at times, although their appearance cannot be counted on. During some years bluefish chase large schools of poggies up the Damariscotta, all the way to the town landing. Look for the best action for all three of these fish in late July and the month of August.

Damariscotta is an attractive town which caters to tourists. The river itself is handsome with mixed growth on moderate hillsides and many sea birds present.

Scale ½" = 1 Mile

Miles

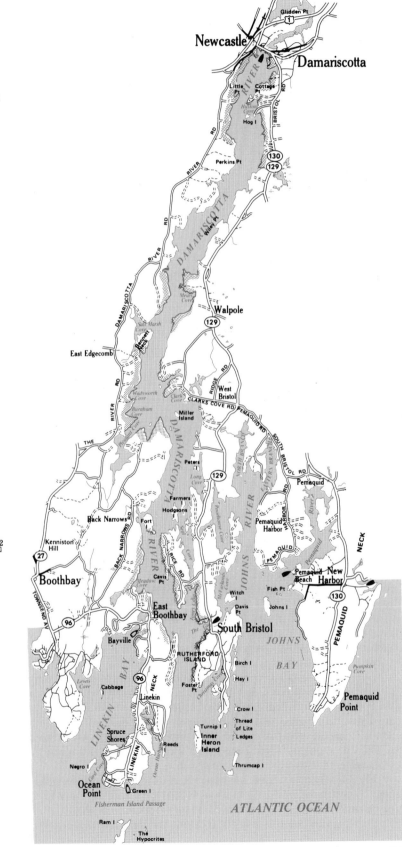

Dead River, North Branch
Chain of Ponds to Eustis

Franklin and Somerset Counties
Maine Atlas maps 28,29

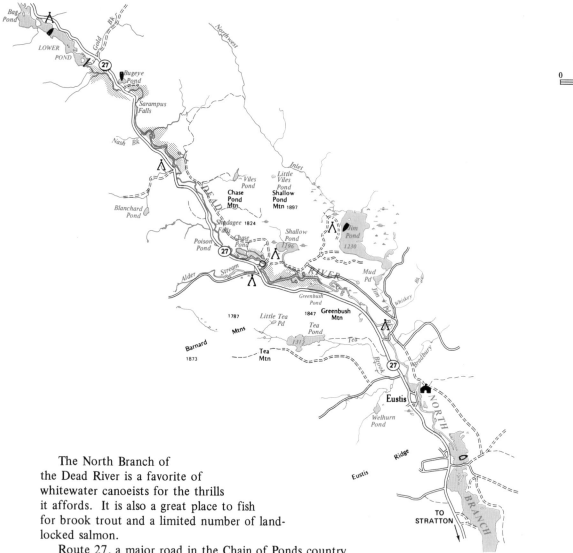

The North Branch of
the Dead River is a favorite of
whitewater canoeists for the thrills
it affords. It is also a great place to fish
for brook trout and a limited number of landlocked salmon.

Route 27, a major road in the Chain of Ponds country
near the Canadian boundary, borders the North Branch. The country
is steep mountains covered with mixed growth, and it's a long way between gas stations in this area.

Generally, the Dead River is rapid, but there are plenty of good, fishable pools.
Good fishing starts just below the dam at the Lower Pond. The upper river is best fished by
wading, although it is difficult on a mostly boulder bottom, with the rocks covered with algae. There
are a number of good pools in the stretch from the dam to where the river crosses under Route 27.
There is another good stretch of water in the area where Alder Stream flows in. This latter section
is smooth-flowing and best fished from a canoe. Any place along the route where you see a pool
or inviting glide may produce a good fish.

Fly hatches on the river are sparse, but olive and brown nymphs work well as do standard streamers. Expect trout in the 10 to 14-inch class with an occasional 1½ to 2 pound fish. The salmon tend
to be small ones that have dropped down from Chain of Ponds.

Best time to fish this country is during the month of June well into July.

Dead River, South Branch
Stratton to Rangeley

Franklin and Somerset Counties
Maine Atlas maps 28, 29

Route 16 offers plenty of easy access to this medium-sized stream. It is an inviting and easy to fish river. Even so, it gets light fishing pressure.

Brook trout are the primary gamefish in the South Branch and fish in the 8 to 12-inch category are the average. There doesn't seem to be much insect activity on the stream, so dry fly fishing tends to be spotty. Streamers, bucktails, wets, and nymphs will all produce, as well as bait. There are plenty of attractive pools separated by long riffles. Wading tends to be difficult because of the rocky bottom.

Best fishing is middle of June to middle of July. The fish are likely to be in any pool you happen to stop at but the area just above the inlet of Flagstaff Lake seems to be a favorite with local people.

The surrounding country is mostly alder flats as this is a surprisingly non-mountainous area lying between Saddleback and Bigelow.

Scale ½" = 1 Mile

Miles

15

Dennys River
Meddybemps to Dennysville

Washington County
Maine Atlas maps 26, 27, 36

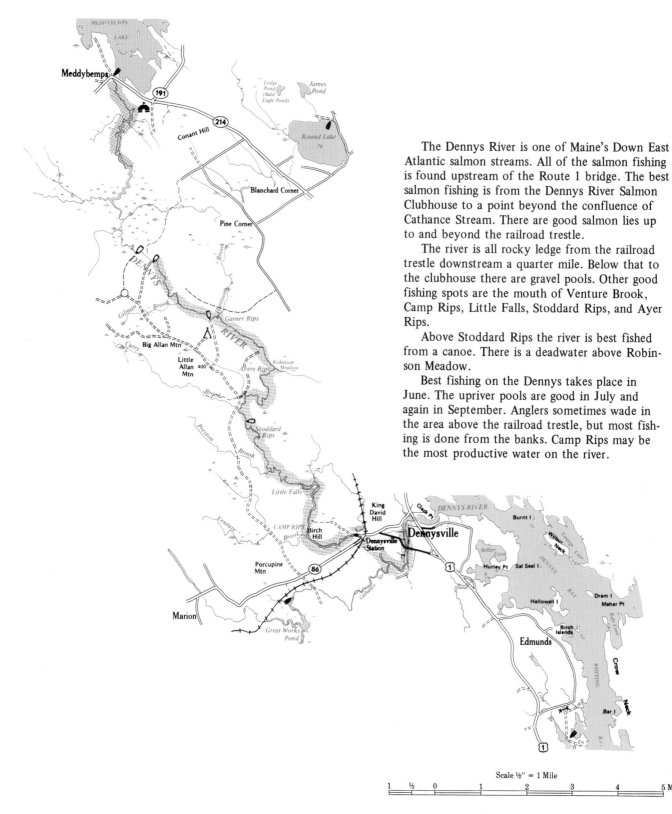

The Dennys River is one of Maine's Down East Atlantic salmon streams. All of the salmon fishing is found upstream of the Route 1 bridge. The best salmon fishing is from the Dennys River Salmon Clubhouse to a point beyond the confluence of Cathance Stream. There are good salmon lies up to and beyond the railroad trestle.

The river is all rocky ledge from the railroad trestle downstream a quarter mile. Below that to the clubhouse there are gravel pools. Other good fishing spots are the mouth of Venture Brook, Camp Rips, Little Falls, Stoddard Rips, and Ayer Rips.

Above Stoddard Rips the river is best fished from a canoe. There is a deadwater above Robinson Meadow.

Best fishing on the Dennys takes place in June. The upriver pools are good in July and again in September. Anglers sometimes wade in the area above the railroad trestle, but most fishing is done from the banks. Camp Rips may be the most productive water on the river.

Scale ½" = 1 Mile

1   ½   0   1   2   3   4   5 Miles

Duck Brook
Harrington Lake to Brighton Deadwater

Piscataquis County
Maine Atlas map 50

There are hefty landlocked salmon caught each year in this fairly small stream. The best fishing is in May with good fishing in June as well.

Harrington Lake is a somewhat remote location near Baxter State Park, reached by crossing the West Branch of the Penobscot at Big Eddy onto the Telos Road. The stream banks are heavily brushed in as the flow coming out of Harrington Lake is controlled.

Best fishing sites are just below the dam and just below Duck Pond. Camping is possible at the Harrington Lake campsite and Duck Pond campsite on the Frost Pond Road. Duck Brook becomes Ripogenus Stream below Brighton Deadwater.

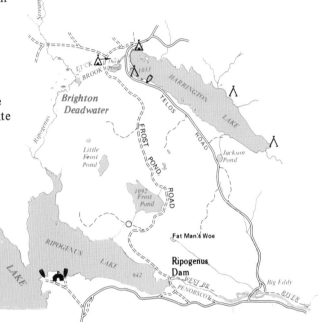

Scale ½″ = 1 Mile

0   1   2

Miles

Ducktrap River
Lincolnville

Waldo County
Maine Atlas map 14

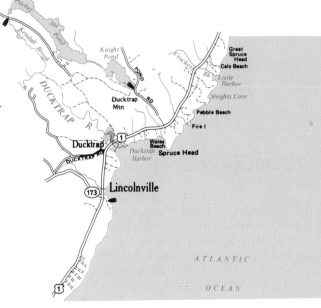

The Ducktrap River might be just another inconsequential coastal stream except for the fact that it is home to a small run of Atlantic salmon. Busy coastal U.S. Route 1 passes over the small stream that is not even noticed by most people. During much of the season the salmon will lie just outside the river in a shallow bar area.

While there is no need for a boat here, a canoe or car topper may be launched from a beach area reached by driving down a road just below the west side of the river. The road is rough, but passable by high-bodied passenger cars.

The times to fish the Ducktrap are in the month of June and again in September. The best fishing is either just off the mouth of the river or on the bend just above Route 1.

Scale ½″ = 1 Mile

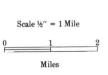

0   1   2

Miles

Fish River
Portage Lake to St. Froid Lake

Aroostook County
Maine Atlas maps 63, 64

This section of the Fish River offers a quick canoe/fishing trip through attractive wooded hills.

During the early spring there are a few lake trout here in the 5- to 6-pound range, but they quickly drop back into the lake. The best time to fish is late May and the month of June. The brook trout range 8 to 12-inches and the land-locked salmon get up to 4 pounds.

Scale ½" = 1 Mile

Miles

Fish River Lake to Portage Lake

This section of the Fish River flows through a dense spruce forest. Highland Camps is located on the river and makes guides available to fish this section. Best fishing is during May and June for 10 to 12 inch brook trout and landlocked salmon up to 4 pounds. Access to Eagle Lake is via Route 11. As most of the river is remote, it makes a good canoe trip. There are many sections which can be waded, although the bottom is rocky and slippery.

Eagle Lake to Fort Kent ⇨

Aroostook County
Maine Atlas map 67

Eagle Lake has excellent landlocked salmon fishing and many of these fish run up and down the river. Brook trout range 10 to 12 inches and the landlocks get to 4 pounds. Sly Brook Road provides good access to the upper reaches of the river from Route 161 out of Fort Kent. There is canoe access at Soldier Pond, a small town, and at Fish River Falls. Canoes must be portaged at Lower Fish Falls. The scenery is very attractive in this river section and the fishing can be rated from good in May to very good in June.

Scale ½″ = 1 Mile

Miles

Grand Lake Stream

West Grand Lake to Big Lake

Washington County
Maine Atlas map 35

During the winter, landlocked salmon group in Grand Lake Stream below the dam to West Grand Lake and thus offer some of the prime opening day fishing found in the state. Of course, this concentration of fish lends itself to crowding.

Other than the opening week flurry, the best fishing in Grand Lake Stream is now in June and two to three pound salmon are common. The dam controls the flow of clean, clear water over a gravel and rock bottom and most people wade, although there are lies in pools which cannot be reached by wading and a canoe is needed. The pool below the dam is a favorite. The stretch of water beside the state fish hatchery in the center of the village is productive. A road which leads from the Georgia-Pacific Picnic Ground parallels the river along the north side and the pool located at the picnic ground is another good fishing spot.

There are sporting camps and campgrounds located in Grand Lake Stream Village which is about 30 miles northwest of Calais.

Scale ½″ = 1 Mile

Miles

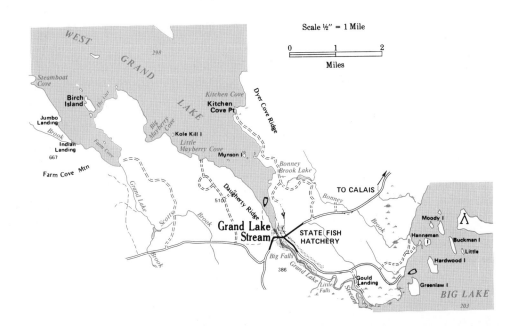

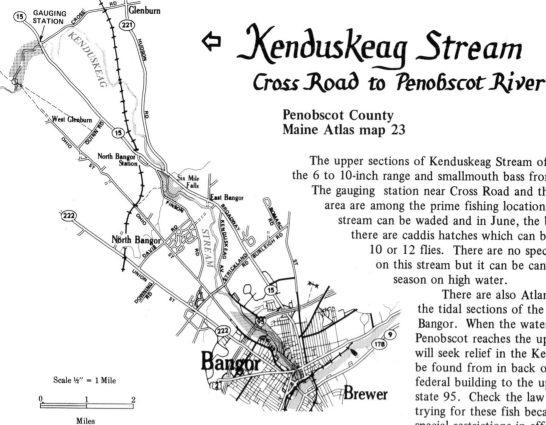

⬅ Kenduskeag Stream
Cross Road to Penobscot River

Penobscot County
Maine Atlas map 23

The upper sections of Kenduskeag Stream offer brook trout in the 6 to 10-inch range and smallmouth bass from 2 to 3 pounds. The gauging station near Cross Road and the Six Mile Falls area are among the prime fishing locations. Sections of the stream can be waded and in June, the best time to fish it, there are caddis hatches which can be imitated with size 10 or 12 flies. There are no specific landing points on this stream but it can be canoed early in the season on high water.

There are also Atlantic salmon found in the tidal sections of the stream in downtown Bangor. When the water temperature in the Penobscot reaches the upper 60s, the salmon will seek relief in the Kenduskeag. Fish will be found from in back of the post office and federal building to the upstream side of Interstate 95. Check the law book carefully before trying for these fish because there may be special restrictions in effect.

Kennebago River ⮕
Kennebago Lake to Oquossoc

Franklin and Oxford Counties
Maine Atlas map 28

The Kennebago is becoming well-known for its mid-September run of large landlocked salmon, sometimes producing fish over 8 pounds. Probably the most famous fishing area is Steep Bank Pool. The salmon will hold in this deep pool and the two pools located just below it, waiting for high water to move upstream on. This section of the Kennebago, and the upstream portions, are best fished from the bank or by wading. Fishing here can also be good in June and early July with salmon up to 2 pounds and brook trout in the 10 to 12-inch range. Later on brook trout can be caught at the mouth of Whetstone Brook, which is best reached by putting a canoe in at the Route 16 bridge.

Access to the Kennebago for the general public is over a gravel road off Route 16 on the east side of the river. This road can be in bad condition and may prove impassable for low-slung vehicles. To get to the upper reaches of the river, drive to the end of this road and follow the foot path through the woods about 100 yards to reach a private road leading to Kennebago Lake.

Fly hatches on this river seem to be sporadic for both mayflies and caddis flies. There is some gravel bottom which makes for easy wading, but much of the river is slippery rock.

20

Kennebec River

Overview

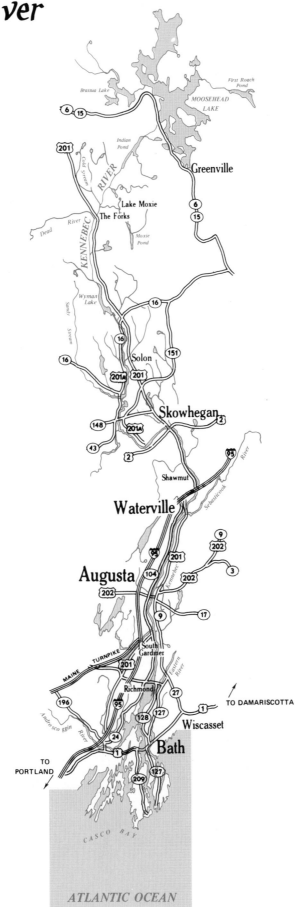

Brassua Lake

First Roach Pond

MOOSEHEAD LAKE

6 15

Indian Pond

201

RIVER

Greenville

6 15

Lake Moxie

The Forks

Dead River

Cold Stream

KENNEBEC RIVER

Moxie Pond

Wyman Lake

16

Sandy Stream

16

151

Solon

16

201A 201

Skowhegan

2

148

201A

95 River

43

2

Shawmut

Sebasticook River

Waterville

9

202

95

201

Augusta

104

Kennebec

202

3

202

17

9

MAINE TURNPIKE

South Gardiner

201

Eastern River

27

Richmond

TO DAMARISCOTTA

196

95

127

1

Androscoggin River

128

Wiscasset

24

1

Bath

TO PORTLAND

209

127

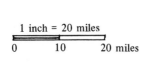

1 inch = 20 miles

0   10   20 miles

CASCO BAY

ATLANTIC OCEAN

21

Kennebec River
East Outlet & West Outlet

Somerset and Piscataquis Counties
Maine Atlas maps 40,41

The West Outlet of the Kennebec is 8 miles long from Moosehead Lake to Indian Pond and is largely a series of interconnected ponds. It is canoeable only at high water. The East Outlet is 3 miles long and contains some very sharp rapids, but is always canoeable. The main attraction of both outlets is the landlocked salmon and the best time of year to fish for them is the month of June, although May can also be productive.

Many anglers fish right from the deck of the East Outlet dam which stands about 20 feet over the river and they lose a lot of fish as they crank them up from the water. When the river is running low on weekends (because the dam is shut down), the downstream pools can be waded. A road goes down the west bank of the East Outlet and is good for passenger vehicles for only half its length. About 6/10 of a mile down this road from Route 15 is an immense pool, several hundred yards long, with a good gravel beach. It offers easy flyfishing conditions and classic salmon water. The south side of the Route 15 bridge is another spot to try.

The West Outlet is much smaller than the East in terms of water flow. There is a campground located just north of the Route 15 bridge where a hand-carried boat or canoe can be launched to fish the quiet water just below the bridge. A good gravel road goes down the west side of the river offering easy access to much of the river. After the river flows through Long Pond it forms a nice pool with a canoe access about 3 miles from Route 15. There is plenty of fishable flatwater below this section.

Scale ½″ = 1 Mile

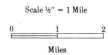

Miles

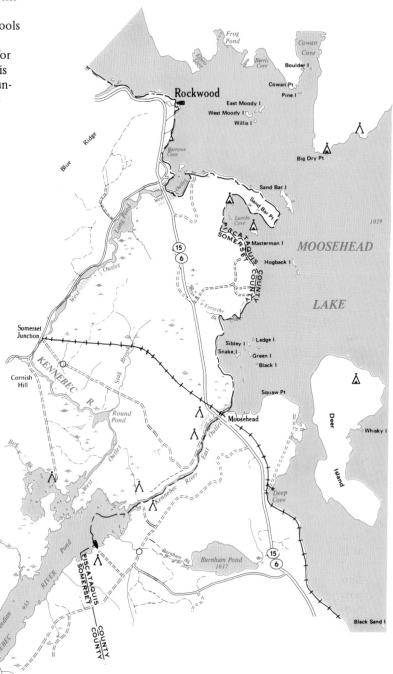

22

Somerset County
Maine Atlas maps 30,40

Rainbow trout, landlocked salmon, and brook trout can be caught in this upper portion of the Kennebec River which is a favorite of canoeists and kayakers.

The area of the river just below the village, where the Kennebec is joined by the Dead River, is all flat fast water but with enough large boulders to give fish holding places. Water levels here are controlled by the Central Maine Power dam at Indian Pond and fluctuate greatly. When the river is down it is easily wadeable, but when the water starts coming up you want to head for shore fast. Generally, you can inquire at local stores to find out what the water levels will be. It is worth investigating the junction area of the Dead River upstream for the first several hundred yards to see if fish are holding in any number of likely riffles and backwaters.

During July, when the water level is low, it's possible to walk up the banks of the river for miles. A trip up the north shore of the Kennebec is a good idea. When you get to Cold Stream follow it upstream a distance and you will locate a number of good pools where brook trout are likely to be found.

The bottom of the river is quite rocky and slippery but easily wadeable during low flows. When the river is running full, the fishing is probably not worth bothering with. There are caddis fly hatches in late June. Access is by Route 201 out of Skowhegan.

Scale ½″ = 1 Mile

0   1   2
Miles

Wyman Dam to Solon ➡

Somerset County
Maine Atlas Map 30

A prime opening day spot in the state is the fast water below Wyman Dam, one of the few places that can be counted upon to be ice-free at that time of year, even with drifts of snow still lying on the ground. Often some of the opening day fish will be lunker landlocked salmon or rainbow trout in the over 7-pound range.

Because water coming out of Wyman Dam is from the bottom of the the lake, this is one of the few areas in Maine that offers good fishing right into August with the action picking up again in September. Some of the best fishing is found right below the dam and can be reached from Route 201 in Moscow by turning onto the road that is clearly marked as leading to the dam.

There is a rough but adequate area to launch boats from just off Route 16 on the west side of Bingham below the bridge. It is also possible to put in a canoe on the east side of the Route 201A bridge in Solon. This is another good fishing area where brown trout may be present. Good places to fish exist right above and below this bridge and there are both caddis and mayfly hatches in June. Wading is possible here during low flow periods.

23

Kennebec River
Skowhegan to Shawmut Dam

Somerset and Kennebec Counties
Maine Atlas map 21

Smallmouth bass fishing is excellent in this all-flatwater section of the Kennebec River. There also are good numbers of white and yellow perch as well as an occasional landlocked salmon.

A high quality boat launch area is located on Route 2 outside Skowhegan next to an attractive picnic area. Rapidly flowing water about a half mile above this launching area might be worth exploring by wading and casting for smallmouths. Everything downstream really requires a canoe or a boat to fish adequately, other than from bridges. While a canoe could be put in at any of the bridge crossings, the Skowhegan boat launch is the only real access area, until near the Shawmut dam downstream.

There is excellent fishing around the islands a mile or so below the Skowhegan boat launch area. Some of these islands have eroded sand cliffs on their upper ends where hundreds of swallows have dug nest holes.

The terrain is a flat mixture of woodlands and farms. While the scenery is not particularly interesting, the fishing can be fast for bass in the 2 to 3 pound range.

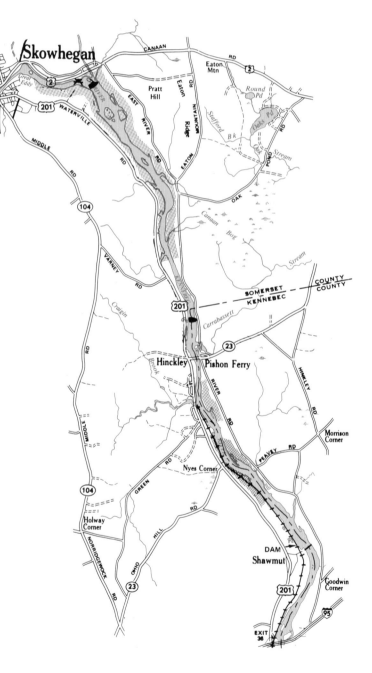

Scale ½″ = 1 Mile

0   1   2

Miles

24

Waterville to Augusta

Kennebec County
Maine Atlas maps 12, 13, & 21

Roads closely follow both sides of the Kennebec in this area but generally are far enough away so one could easily imagine being in a wild region rather than one of the most heavily settled sections of Maine.

Boat access is via one of two state-sponsored launches located on Route 104 on the west side of the river. One launch area is in Sidney and the other about a mile and a half below Waterville. It's possible to launch a canoe or hand-carried boat from Fort Halifax Park off Route 201 in Winslow. Water flows here may be too rapid and shallow to allow paddling or motoring upstream to return to the park, so it's best to plan a take-out down river.

Smallmouth bass are the prime attraction in this section of the river which also contains white and yellow perch. There is also the possibility of picking up a stray landlocked salmon or brown trout.

The banks leading down to the river are quite steep. This saved much of the riverfront from development other than the railroad tracks that follow closely the east shore.

The month of June is probably prime time to fish this section although late September is also a good time to try for the smallmouth which frequently hit 3 pounds or better.

Note: during high water the river runs fast for the first 3 miles below Waterville and it may be impossible to take a boat or canoe back upstream without a motor.

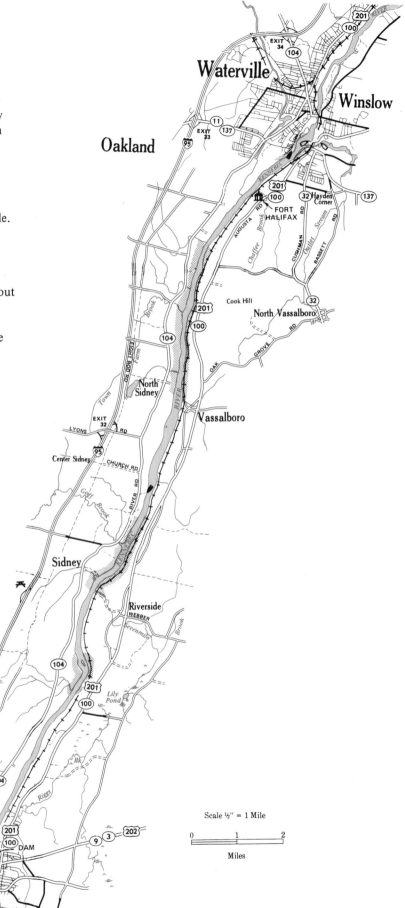

Scale ½″ = 1 Mile

0   1   2

Miles

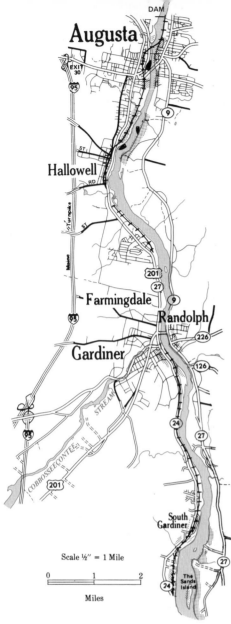

Kennebec River
Augusta to South Gardiner

Kennebec County
Maine Atlas map 12

Variety is the word for those who fish the Kennebec River below the Augusta dam. Among the species found are striped bass, alewives, brown trout, landlocked salmon, Atlantic salmon, smallmouth bass, pickerel, white perch, yellow perch, eels and carp.

Most of the fishing attention is focused on the striper run (late May through early July) and the Atlantic salmon, found primarily just below the dam and beneath the bridges in Augusta. Fishing below the dam, a good spot for all the varieties of fish, has to be done from a boat as factories on either side of the river prevent easy access. By walking through the parking lots located on the west side of the river, downstream fishing in the area of bridges is possible from shore.

This section of the Kennebec is well endowed with boat launch areas. There is a launch in Augusta on the east side of the river, just under the high bridge. It is reached by driving down Arsenal Street and turning right at City Hall. Another launch is located in downtown Hallowell just off Route 201. There is a third in Gardiner, just below the inlet of the Cobbossee Stream. The Cobbossee Stream inlet is a hot spot to fish in June for white perch and for stripers. The stripers tend to be school fish in the 2 to 5 pound range.

A number of brown trout in the 3 to 5 pound range are taken in the river each spring. The Kennebec has the only sizeable population of carp in the state and there is good fishing for them in The Sands Island area of South Gardiner where niblet corn is a good bait.

Richmond to Merrymeeting Bay

Lincoln and Sagadahoc Counties
Maine Atlas maps 6,12

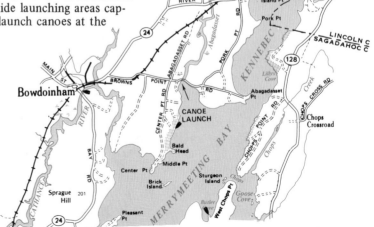

Some of the largest tidal marshes in the state are found in the Swan Island-Merrymeeting Bay portion of the Kennebec River. A scenery-rich section of the river, chances are good here for seeing a bald eagle and waterfowls abound. The waters of the Merrymeeting were once badly polluted, but they are much cleaner now.

Shad are a possibility in the area and are expected to become abundant in the years ahead. Good runs of fish are already reported in the Cathance and Abagadasset Rivers starting in early June. Also present from mid-May to mid-July are school-sized stripers, often found feeding around various rocky points.

There are excellent paved boat launching areas off Route 24 in Richmond and on the Cathance in Bowdoinham. These are all tide launching areas capable of handling any size boat. It is also possible to launch canoes at the Abagadasset from Brown's Point Road.

Merrymeeting Bay is full of carp up to 15 pounds which are mostly ignored by anglers. Sometimes they are picked up on worms, but chumming them with whole kernel corn is the most effective method of catching these fish.

Tides in Merrymeeting Bay are substantial, 6 feet or more, and follow the coastal tide by about 3 hours.

Scale ½" = 1 Mile

Miles

26

Bath to Atlantic Ocean

Sagadahoc and Cumberland Counties
Maine Atlas map 6

It takes a solid boat and a motor of at least 10 horse-power to handle the immensely strong tidal currents of this section of the Kennebec. It might take only 45 minutes to make a boat trip from the Bath landing to Popham Beach going with the tide in a powerful boat, but it would take an hour and a half to come back.

This section of the Kennebec is famous for its striped bass fishing, from schoolies up to 50-pounders. The fishing tends to be spotty, but those who get into the fish can enjoy furious action. Bluefish also enter the river, often moving up to at least Phippsburg. Much of the best striper fishing in the Kennebec is done at night, letting live eels swim in back eddies. Probably the most famous fishing area is right at the mouth of the river at Popham Beach where stripers, bluefish, mackerel and harbor pollock are taken.

The scenery is spectacular all along this section of river. Bath Iron Works is located on the west side of the river at Bath and immense warships are often docked there. Once past Doubling Point the green hills are largely undeveloped except for such scenic structures as light-houses.

An excellent boat launch is located in Bath about a mile north of Route One. Just follow the waterfront and find it next to the city's sewage treatment plant. There is a rough launch in Phippsburg from off a dirt road across from the post office. There is a part tide area across from Fort Popham where a small boat can be launched, but be careful of the sand and mud.

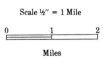

Scale ½″ = 1 Mile

Miles

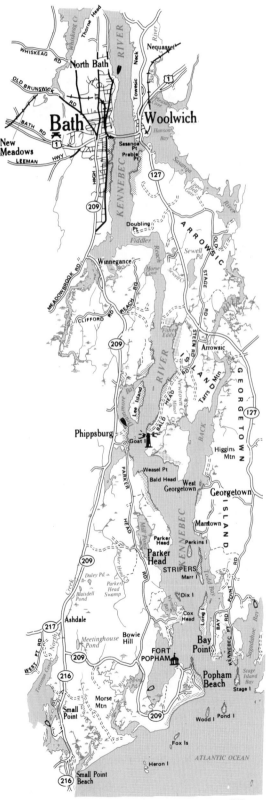

Little Madawaska River
Madawaska Lake to Aroostook River

Aroostook County
Maine Atlas maps 64, 65, & 68

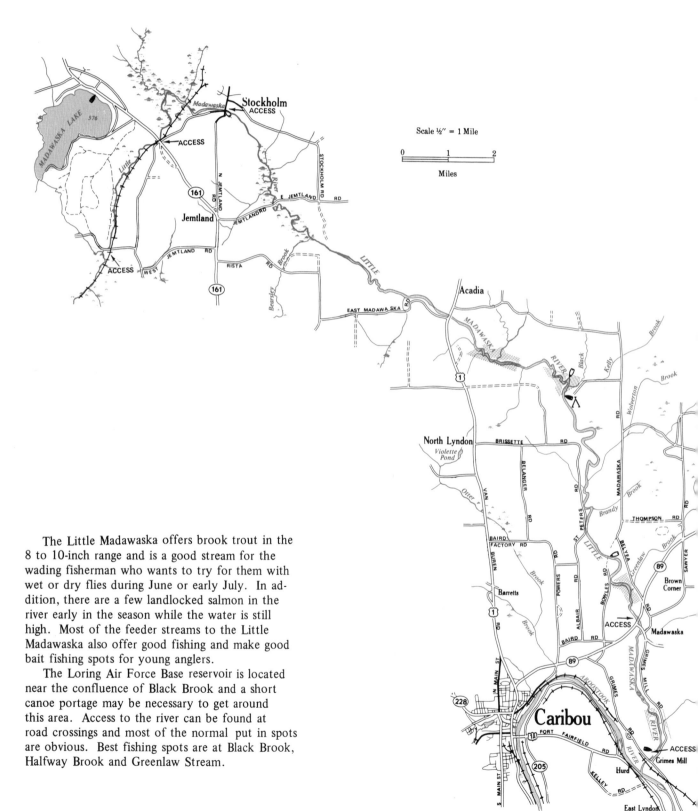

The Little Madawaska offers brook trout in the 8 to 10-inch range and is a good stream for the wading fisherman who wants to try for them with wet or dry flies during June or early July. In addition, there are a few landlocked salmon in the river early in the season while the water is still high. Most of the feeder streams to the Little Madawaska also offer good fishing and make good bait fishing spots for young anglers.

The Loring Air Force Base reservoir is located near the confluence of Black Brook and a short canoe portage may be necessary to get around this area. Access to the river can be found at road crossings and most of the normal put in spots are obvious. Best fishing spots are at Black Brook, Halfway Brook and Greenlaw Stream.

Little Ossipee River
Newfield to Ossipee Mills

York County
Maine Atlas map 2

A brown trout fishery exists in the Little Ossipee River, mostly due to annual stocking. Naturally, the fish are not large, mostly in the 8 to 10-inch range, with occasional reports of larger fish.

The best fishing on this small stream is May until mid-June when it heats up too much and the fish flee. The entire stretch from the Newfield Bridge to the Route 5 bridge in Ossipee Mills offers good fishing. The river is easily waded and features undercut banks, lots of riffles and a few deep pools. During late May there are sporadic hatches of mayflies and caddis flies and sometimes the trout can be found feeding on top.

A good canoe day trip, combined with fishing, can be made from North Shapleigh to Ossipee Mills. This passes through a mixture of marsh, flatwater, quickwater and moderate riffles during May while the water remains high. Put in at Davis Brook in North Shapleigh. Take out is just below the Route 5 bridge.

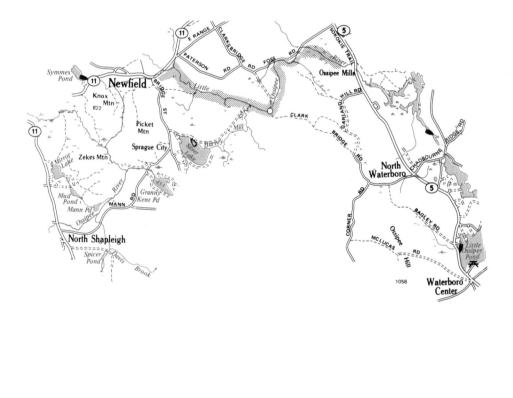

Scale ½" = 1 Mile

Machias River
Fifth Machias Lake to First Machias Lake

Washington and Hancock Counties
Maine Atlas map 35

Brook trout is the prime attraction for this stretch of the river, but there are smallmouth bass and pickerel available as well. The trout tend to be in the 10 to 16-inch range and will be found in all the fast water areas early in April and at the mouths of brooks after May 30. Many sections of the river can be waded and there are mayfly hatches from the middle of May to the middle of June. The best fishing is in Fifth Lake Stream and Third Lake Stream.

This is a wilderness area and one of Maine's better canoe trips. Best river running conditions are found in June and some of the rapids should be scouted before running them although there are no Class IV rapids.

Access to the area is by taking the Stud Mill Road turn off and traveling Road Num

Scale ½" = 1 Mile

1   ½   0   1   2   3   4   5 Miles

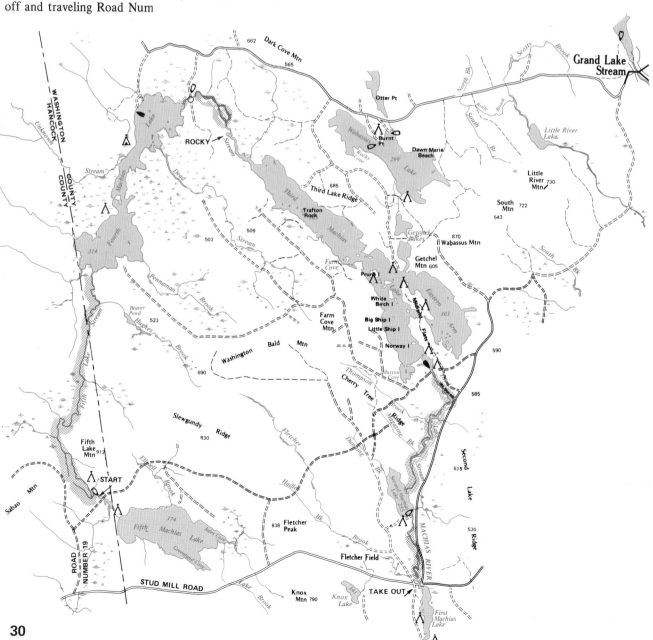

Route 9 to Smith Landing

Washington County
Maine Atlas map 25,26

Here's another good Washington County canoe trip offering good fishing for brook trout in the 10 to 14-inch class, and the bonus possibility of encountering Atlantic salmon.

Start the trip where Route 9 crosses the river. Watch out for the stretch of whitewater at Little Falls near Upper Buck Mountain; it can be run at some levels. There is a definite portage necessary at Holmes Falls. The take out is at Smith Landing where there is a road which leads to Route 192 and Northfield.

The brook trout fishing will be best during the second two weeks of May and the first two weeks of June. Once warm water settles in, look for the brook trout only around the mouths of inlet streams.

Scale ½" = 1 Mile

0   1   2

Miles

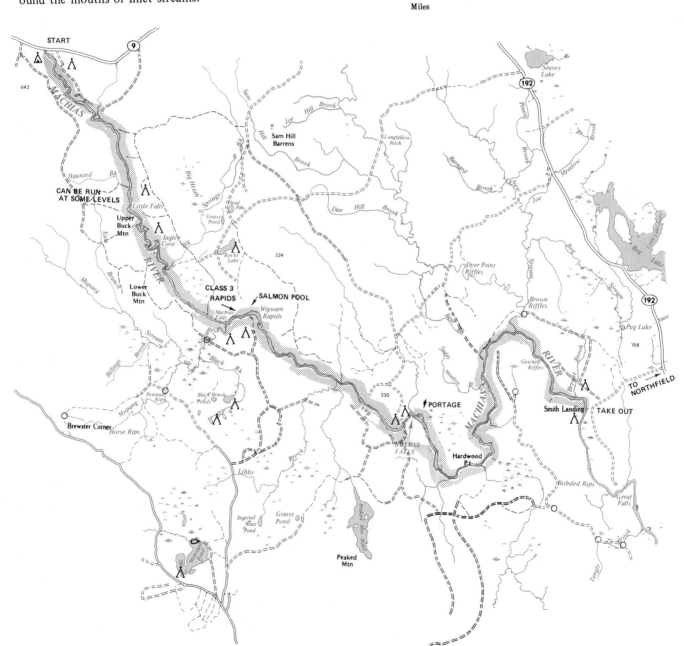

Machias & East Machias Rivers
Northfield to Atlantic Ocean

Washington County
Maine Atlas map 26

These two river sections are prime areas for Atlantic salmon fishing with the peak coming in June.

On the East Machias there is good fishing above the Route 191 bridge at Jacksonville. Other good fishing is found above and below the two Route 1 bridges. This is all bank fishing and canoes are not used. There are two popular salmon lies at Chase Mill Pool, one on either side of the river. Fisherman here use mostly wet flies and floating lines. In the upstream areas, Great Meadow Riffles and Munsun Rips are possible places to look for salmon. Between Hadley and Second Lake, salmon may be found at Wigwam Riffles and Crooked Pitch but these are not considered prime fishing areas.

On the main Machias, in the town of Machias, the area right behind Helen's Restaurant in town at the foot of the gorge is a favorite spot. Salmon are found from there to the end of the fairgrounds. Munson's Pitch is a good holding pool and the railroad bridge at Whitneyville is another good bet. There are good salmon lies from under the Route 1A bridge to the old dam site upstream.

Scale ½" = 1 Mile

0   1   2
Miles

Machias River, West Branch
Cranberry Lakes to Machias River

Washington County
Maine Atlas maps 25, 35

Scale ½" = 1 Mile

1   ½   0   1   2   3   4   5 Miles

There are 10 to 14-inch brook trout in the West Branch of the
Machias River from May to the middle of June and the best way to
get to them is by canoe. From Route 9 take the road leading to
the Cranberry Lakes and cross the upper lake to the stream. The
first part of the West Branch flows through meadows and then it
changes to typically Maine rocky river conditions. The take out is
at the bridge that carries the CCC road over the river.

Wading is possible in considerable stretches of the river and there
are mayfly hatches in late May and the first two weeks of June. The
best pools are located at Rolford Dam and the mouth of Ingalls
Brook.

Magalloway River
Parmachenee to Aziscohos Lake

Oxford County
Maine Atlas map 28

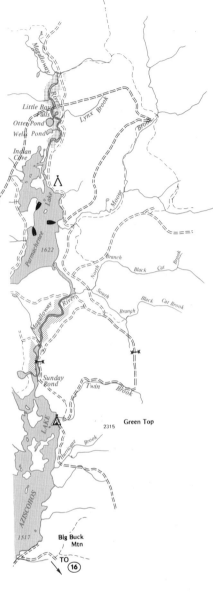

This is a remote but well-known stretch of water respected for its brook trout fishing. Best fishing is in the month of June and there are fly hatches.

Access to this area is not easy. To reach the upper section of the river, one good possibility is to transport a canoe into Parmachenee Lake by airplane and canoe past the flatwater section just above the lake. To reach the lower end of the river you can launch a boat on the lower end of Aziscohos Lake from Route 16 and motor to the upper end of the lake and walk up the road on the east side of the river. There is also good fishing for brookies and the occasional landlocked salmon where the Magalloway empties into Aziscohos.

The best known pool is just below Little Boys Falls which gained fame when it was fished in the 50s by President Eisenhower. Don't neglect the water just above the falls either. Trout in this area run in the 8 to 12-inch range with the occasional 2-pounder showing up.

Scale ½″ = 1 Mile

Miles

Mattawamkeag River
Kingman to Mattawamkeag

Penobscot County
Maine Atlas map 44

Scale ½″ = 1 Mile

Miles

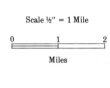

The lower section of the river near Mattawamkeag Wilderness Park offers beauty and an excellent pool lined with huge granite formations. Good brook trout fishing has been the mainstay of this section for many years, but the release of Atlantic salmon above the Veazie Dam on the Penobscot has added a whole new dimension.

From Kingman to Mattawamkeag the river is very dangerous for canoeing as there are huge rapids in the spring.

Gordon Brook is the prime pool and the trout are in the 8 to 12-inch range. Best fishing is in June when there are mayfly and caddis hatches. There is more good fishing water along Mattawamkeag Wilderness Park reached by taking the road out of Mattawamkeag that comes off of Route 2 and runs along the south side of the river.

Mattawamkeag River, West Branch
Mattawamkeag Lake to Haynesville

Aroostook County
Maine Atlas maps 52,53

The countryside along the West Branch of the Mattawamkeag ranges from hardwood ridges to swamp land. The river offers good early fishing for brook trout in the foot long category and an occasional landlocked salmon. Best fishing is from May 1 to June 15. Most of the river is too deep for wading except for riffle areas.

The river can be canoed by putting in at Mattawamkeag Lake and taking out at Haynesville. By July it is often too shallow in some areas to float a canoe through.

To find the river take Interstate 95 and then Route 2 to Mattawamkeag Lake or Route 2A to Haynesville. City Camp Landing and The Flats are the most productive fishing areas.

There are smallmouth bass, pickerel and perch in the stretch of the Mattawamkeag just south of Haynesville, with the best fishing early in the season, as the river suffers from low water in summer.

Scale ½" = 1 Mile

0   1   2
Miles

Meduxnekeag River
Meduxnekeag Lake to Houlton

Aroostook County
Maine Atlas map 53

There are some brook trout in the 1½ to 2 pound range in the Meduxnekeag, but it is best known for being the only brown trout river in this section of the state. The browns have taken very well to the Meduxnekeag and there are fish 25 inches long weighing 5 to 6 pounds.

Best fishing is from opening day to mid-June and in September. Wading is moderately difficult over a rocky and gravelly bottom. There are some very deep pools in the river. It is possible to canoe the Meduxnekeag, but only early in the season.

The South Branch of the Meduxnekeag is quite a productive stream in its own right and the two branches produce brookies in the 8 to 12-inch range and browns averaging 16 inches. This is a highly productive fishing water because it is heavy in concentrations of limestone.

You can reach the river by taking Interstate 95 to Houlton and then travelling Route 1 to Route 2 or Route 2A.

Scale ½" = 1 Mile

0   1   2
Miles

35

Millinocket Stream
Millinocket Lake to Millinocket

Penobscot County
Maine Atlas map 43

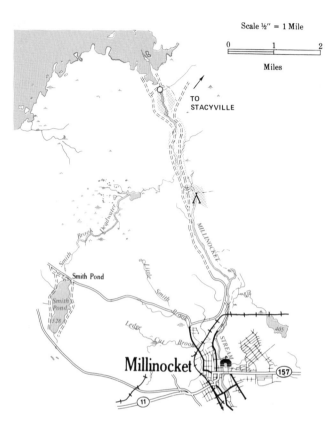

When conditions are good, Millinocket Stream can be a fast producer of landlocked salmon, brook trout and smallmouth bass. June is the best month for the trout and salmon and July is tops for bass.

From Route 157 in Millinocket take the Stacyville Road. A fairly good gravel road follows along the east side of the stream and there is another for part of the way along the west side.

There is little fishing pressure on this stream, especially once the ponds and lakes become ice free. The mouths of small brooks are good places to fish in hot weather. There are good mayfly hatches in June and large caddis flies in late June and July. The bottom cover varies between sand, gravel and rocks; as a result wading conditions can be from easy to impossible. The stream can be canoed by putting in at the dam, but portaging will be necessary at various points.

Two excellent spots to fish are below the dam and at the first big bend in the river. The trout will average 8 to 14 inches with the landlocked salmon going 14 to 20 inches. A bonus in the stream are some jumbo white perch to be found in some of the quieter pools. The river can be fished all the way to the railroad tracks in Millinocket.

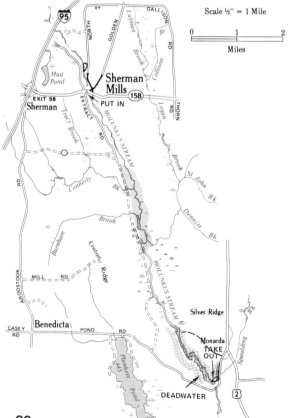

Molunkus Stream
Sherman Mills to Pond Road

Aroostook County
Maine Atlas map 52

Molunkus Stream offers brook trout fishing only early in the season. Fish in the 6 to 12-inch range can be caught in the upper stretches from May 1 to May 15.

Best fishing areas are the deadwater just off the Pond Road in Benedicta and the Burnham Brook inlet. The bottom is gravel and mud and the wading is easy in most places. The lower section of the stream has pickerel and smallmouth bass.

The stream can be canoed by putting in at Route 158 in Sherman Mills and taking out at the Pond Road in Benedicta or along Route 2. There is an exit off Route 95 in nearby Sherman.

Moose River
Bow Trip

Somerset County
Maine Atlas map 39

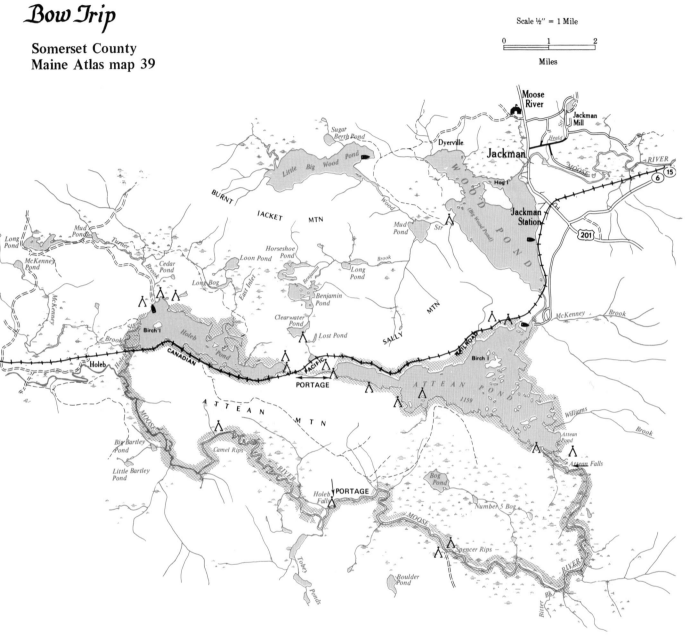

The Moose River Bow Trip is one of Maine's more famous canoe trips and offers good fishing for brook trout and landlocked salmon along the way. The trip could be done in as little as two days to cover the 46 miles involved, but four or five days makes it much more enjoyable and it will take a week if you really want to fish seriously.

You start out on Attean Pond near the Canadian Pacific Railway Bridge, reached via a good road off Route 201 just south of Jackman Station.

The trip goes six miles across Attean Pond to a mile and a half portage over a good trail to Holeb Pond. Once across the pond, you enter Holeb Stream where it is possible to encounter some good sized brook trout. From the pond to Holeb Falls the river is mostly flatwater surrounded by swamp and brush country and does not offer particularly good fishing.

Caution is necessary in the Holeb Falls area. An hour and a quarter from Camel Rips there is a cabin on the right bank. About two miles below, the river divides and you should take the smaller channel to the left, bearing right with the current immediately afterwards. Continue another mile past a still water on the left and just beyond turn left again through the tiny passage when you hear the waterfalls. This will take you to the portage trail leading to the Holeb Falls campsite. The area around Holeb Falls is one of the best to fish for pan-sized brook trout, particularly in June. Probably the best location to fish for landlocked salmon is at Attean Falls about a mile before you get back to Attean Pond.

This trip includes lakes, flatwater, whitewater and falls and everything from swamps to mountains.

37

Moose River

Long Pond to Little Brassua Lake

Somerset County
Maine Atlas map 40

To find this section of the Moose River drive west on Route 15 from Rockwood and turn right onto the road which is located about a half mile before Trout Brook.

The road leads to a bridge which crosses the river. Downstream from this bridge there are excellent pools and riffles which are productive for landlocked salmon. Access both up and down river can be achieved by walking the railroad tracks which closely follow its course.

This river section is generally rocky and there are many car to house-sized boulders which can be used as casting platforms, although there also are locations where wading is possible.

This portion of the Moose is big water and those who are not strong fly casters may be more comfortable fishing with spinning gear. The best time for fishing the area is mid-June.

Brassua Lake to Moosehead Lake

Somerset County
Maine Atlas map 40

Mid-September may be the best time of the year to try for the landlocked salmon that run up this section of the Moose River from Moosehead Lake, just north of the town of Rockwood. The month of June would not be a bad time either and the area just below the dam is a good spot to try on opening day.

For about a mile below the huge earthen dam that backs up Brassua Lake there are rapids and pools which not only harbor salmon but brook trout as well. Many anglers follow Route 15 out of Rockwood and then walk down the dirt road leading to the dam to fish the fast water and pools here. Even during the August doldrums it is possible to find fish in the cool waters coming out of the bottom of the dam. Fish up to 3 or 4 pounds are taken here and streamers and bucktails are the favorite lures.

The lower section of the river is flatwater and boats from the lake often troll up it with tandem streamers, Mooselook Wobblers or other lures.

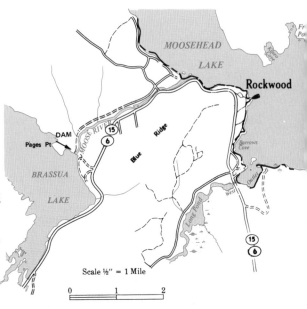

38

Mousam River

Mousam Lake to Springvale

York County
Maine Atlas map 2

There is fair fishing for brook trout up to 10 inches and brown trout up to 12 inches in this section of the Mousam River. Best fishing time is from the start of May to the middle of June.

Among the best pools are Power Line, S-Curve, Emery Mills Bridge, Rapids, Indian's Last Leap and Lunch Pool. There is a story about Indian's Last Leap that goes back to colonial times. According to the story, an Indian was chasing a settler who jumped across the river here, but when the Indian tried it he failed and drowned.

The river bottom is mostly rocky and can be waded in many places. Some fly hatches can be expected in late May and during June.

Access to the river is by Route 109. Canoes can be put in at the Springvale Recreation Area, the S-Curve on Route 109 and the Emery Mills Bridge.

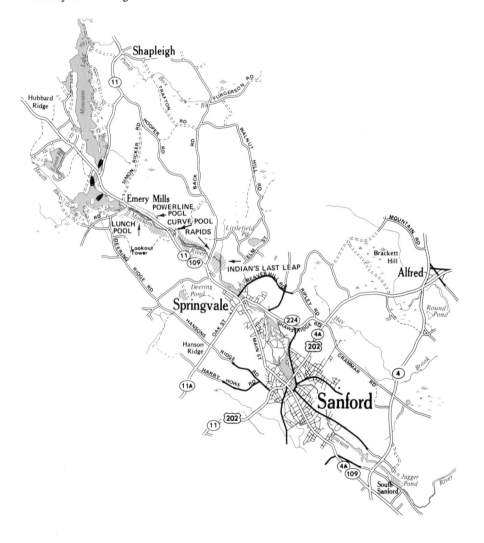

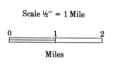

Scale ½" = 1 Mile

Miles

Mousam River
Springvale to Sanford

York County
Maine Atlas map 2

This heavily developed section of river is interspersed with dammed-up ponds. The fishing is for bass, perch and pickerel with a limited number of brown trout available as the remnant of old stockings. Best time to try for the browns is in early spring when they are sometimes caught below the Central Maine Power Company dam at River Street in Sanford. These are good fish in the 2 to 4-pound class.

Stump Pond in Springvale has an excellent population of bass in the 3 to 5-pound range with the best fishing starting in June and remaining fair throughout the summer.

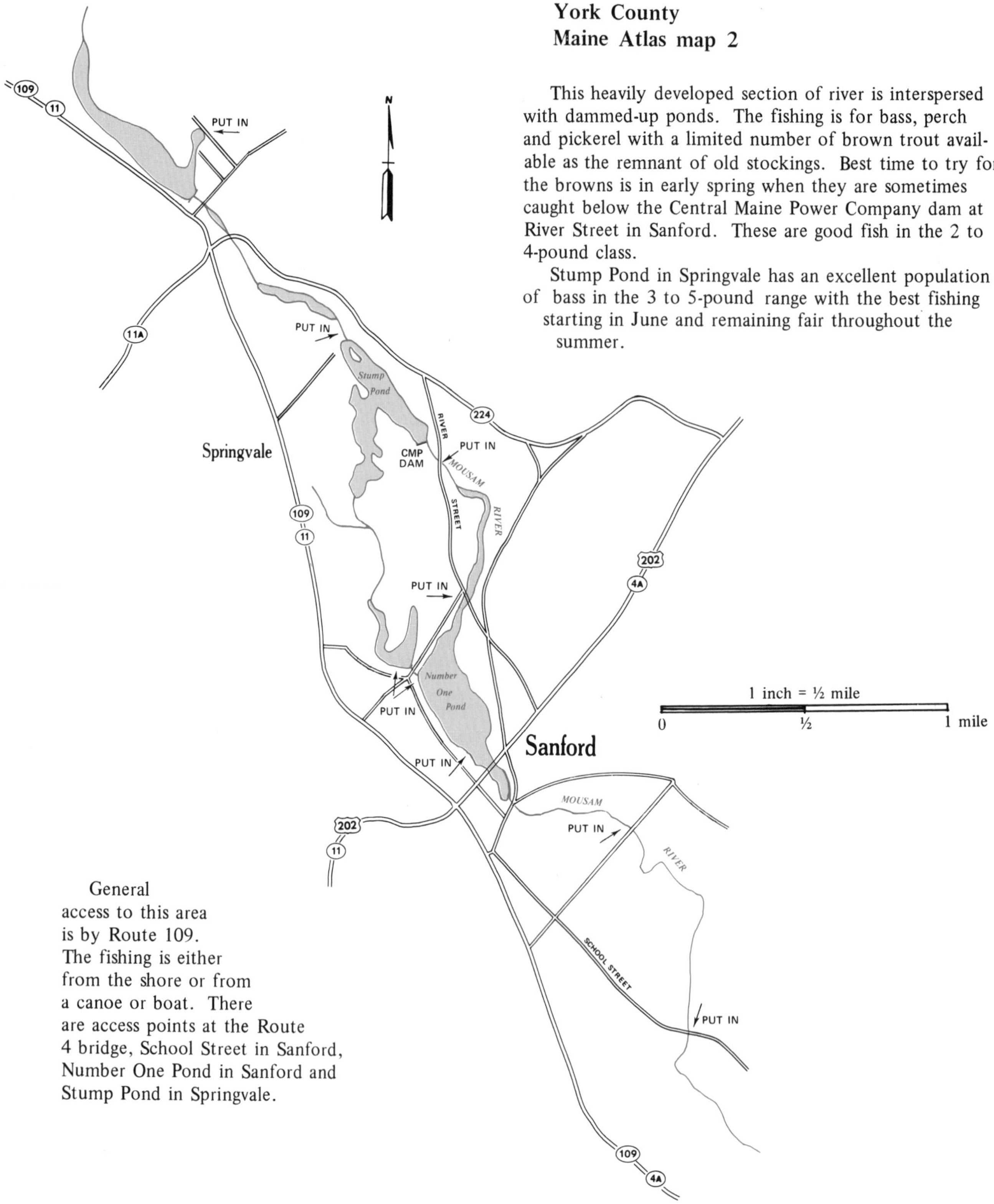

PUT IN

N

109
11

11A

PUT IN

Stump Pond

Springvale

109
11

CMP DAM

224

PUT IN

RIVER STREET

MOUSAM RIVER

PUT IN

202
4A

PUT IN

Number One Pond

1 inch = ½ mile

0   ½   1 mile

Sanford

PUT IN

202
11

MOUSAM

PUT IN

RIVER

SCHOOL STREET

PUT IN

General access to this area is by Route 109. The fishing is either from the shore or from a canoe or boat. There are access points at the Route 4 bridge, School Street in Sanford, Number One Pond in Sanford and Stump Pond in Springvale.

109
4A

40

Estes Lake to West Kennebunk

York County
Maine Atlas map 2

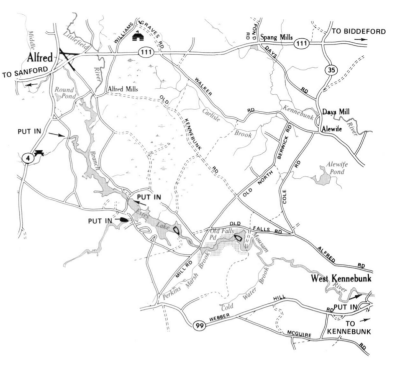

There are some brown and brook trout in this section of the Mousam, but it is mostly a perch, bass, and pickerel stream. Fishing is possible throughout the summer.

You can reach this portion of the river via Route 111 from Biddeford, Routes 4 and 4A from Sanford and Alfred, or Route 99 from Kennebunk. Boats can be put into Estes Lake at Lavalle Bridge. There is a fair boat ramp at the new dam and at the Hay Brook bridge.

Best fishing is in the Old Falls Pond area for both casting and trolling. The shoreline around Estes Lake is quite developed but the lower reaches of the river are wooded.

Scale ½″ = 1 Mile

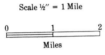

Miles

Route 1 to Atlantic Ocean

York County
Maine Atlas map 3

School-sized stripers and coho salmon up to 20 pounds are the attraction of the lowest portions of the Mousam River. Cohos will be found in the river during the first 3 hours of incoming tide at the Route 9 bridge and the locals fish with sand eels as bait. Stripers in the 2 to 5 pound class are found from the mouth of the river up to the railroad bridge.

The bottom is sandy and can be waded, but it is better to use a boat which can be put in where the Route 9 bridge crosses Back Creek. The best fishing time is July and August.

Scale ½″ = 1 Mile

Miles

Nahmakanta Stream
Nahmakanta Lake to Pemadumcook Lake

Piscataquis and Penobscot Counties
Maine Atlas map 42

   This remote stream is accessible by auto over a road that originates near Bear Brook on Route 11, about 17 miles southwest of Millinocket. The last 4 miles are over a rough, unimproved road. An alternate access would be to fly in to Nahmakanta Lake.

   The stream is good for brook trout in 8 to 15-inch range with a smattering of landlocked salmon up to 20 inches. The best salmon fishing is in the lower reaches. Some fishermen will fish all of the many pools located along the six mile long stream, particularly in June. The good fishing lasts well into early July and there are hatches of mayflies and caddis flies throughout the good fishing times. The bottom is rocky and slippery and wading is difficult due to deep pools. It is not a good place for canoes as some places call for portaging or dragging over rocky shoals.

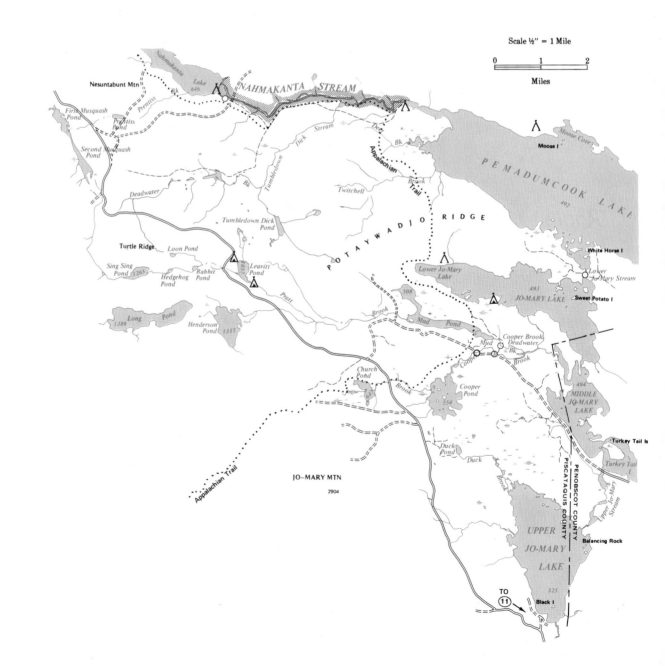

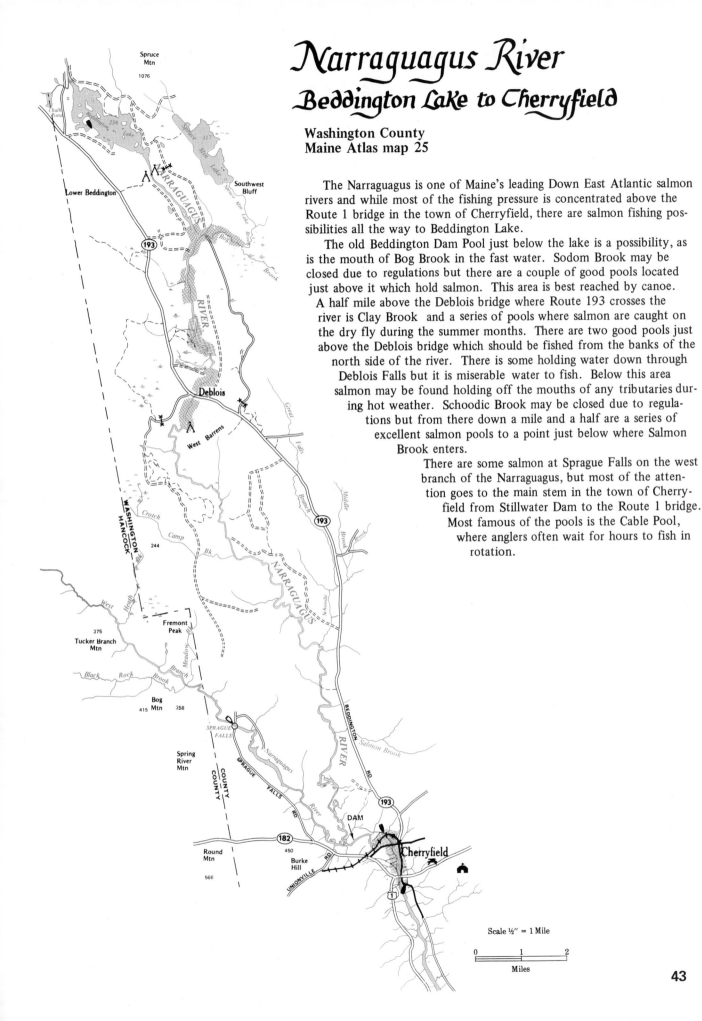

Narraguagus River
Beddington Lake to Cherryfield

Washington County
Maine Atlas map 25

The Narraguagus is one of Maine's leading Down East Atlantic salmon rivers and while most of the fishing pressure is concentrated above the Route 1 bridge in the town of Cherryfield, there are salmon fishing possibilities all the way to Beddington Lake.

The old Beddington Dam Pool just below the lake is a possibility, as is the mouth of Bog Brook in the fast water. Sodom Brook may be closed due to regulations but there are a couple of good pools located just above it which hold salmon. This area is best reached by canoe. A half mile above the Deblois bridge where Route 193 crosses the river is Clay Brook and a series of pools where salmon are caught on the dry fly during the summer months. There are two good pools just above the Deblois bridge which should be fished from the banks of the north side of the river. There is some holding water down through Deblois Falls but it is miserable water to fish. Below this area salmon may be found holding off the mouths of any tributaries during hot weather. Schoodic Brook may be closed due to regulations but from there down a mile and a half are a series of excellent salmon pools to a point just below where Salmon Brook enters.

There are some salmon at Sprague Falls on the west branch of the Narraguagus, but most of the attention goes to the main stem in the town of Cherryfield from Stillwater Dam to the Route 1 bridge. Most famous of the pools is the Cable Pool, where anglers often wait for hours to fish in rotation.

Scale ½" = 1 Mile

0   1   2

Miles

Nesowadnehunk Stream

Nesowadnehunk Lake to Penobscot River, West Branch

**Piscataquis County
Maine Atlas map 50**

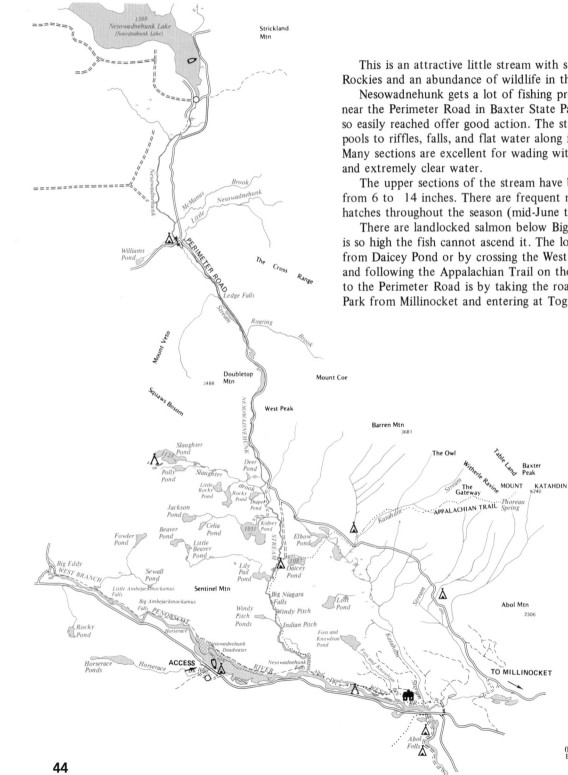

This is an attractive little stream with scenery to rival the Rockies and an abundance of wildlife in the area.

Nesowadnehunk gets a lot of fishing pressure in the pools near the Perimeter Road in Baxter State Park. Other areas not so easily reached offer good action. The stream varies from pools to riffles, falls, and flat water along its 15 mile length. Many sections are excellent for wading with a sand bottom and extremely clear water.

The upper sections of the stream have brook trout ranging from 6 to 14 inches. There are frequent mayfly and caddis hatches throughout the season (mid-June through August).

There are landlocked salmon below Big Niagara Falls which is so high the fish cannot ascend it. The lower end is reached from Daicey Pond or by crossing the West Branch in a canoe and following the Appalachian Trail on the east shore. Access to the Perimeter Road is by taking the road to Baxter State Park from Millinocket and entering at Togue Pond Gate.

Scale ½" = 1 Mile

0   1   2

Miles

Ogunquit River
Ogunquit

**York County
Maine Atlas
map 2**

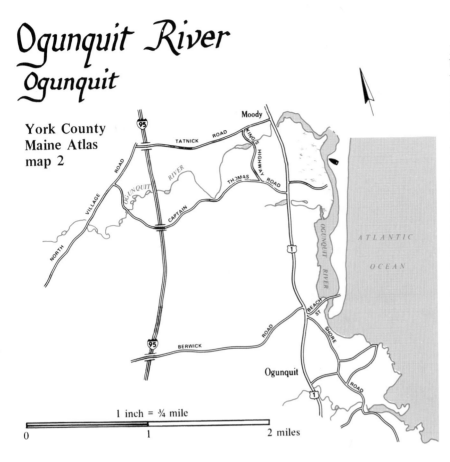

1 inch = ¾ mile

0   1   2 miles

The Ogunquit River offers one of Maine's late fall fisheries for sea-run brown trout and these are good fish which will hit 5 to 6 pounds or more. Some of the fish will be back in September but the best fishing is in October and even into November.

Most of the fishing is done at low tide as the fish are forced into greatly restricted pools and the obvious holding areas become much more apparent. One such place is under the bridge on Beach Street leading to the beach from Route 1. Anglers fish from the shore on the west side both above and below the bridge and above the bridge on the east side.

Perhaps the key is waiting until the water is in the 50 to 60 degree range which is when the fish move up into the river. Anyone considering using a fly rod for these fish should have at least a 9-weight line that sinks fast. Baits and lures along the lines of shrimp and sand eels are productive.

Dress warmly for this fishing because even on a sunny October day the moist salt breeze can be very chilling, particularly to anyone standing in 3 feet of water wearing waders.

Ossipee River
New Hampshire Border to Saco River

**York County
Maine Atlas map 4**

It is possible to catch brown trout in the Ossipee River below the dam in Kezar Falls from May to September, but the best fishing is in late May and early June when there are strong mayfly and caddis fly hatches and both wet and dry flies will take fish.

The Ossipee has excellent riffle and rapid areas and some deep pools with rocky bottoms. Wading is possible in many areas once the water level drops.

The majority of the fish will be recently stocked fish in the 8 to 10-inch range, but there are also hold-overs which will get to 14 inches as well as the occasional old monster which has been around for years.

The section from Kezar Falls to Cornish where it meets the Saco is all good water.

A good canoe day trip can be made by putting in at Effingham Falls on Route 25. There are rapids just over the border which should be scouted.

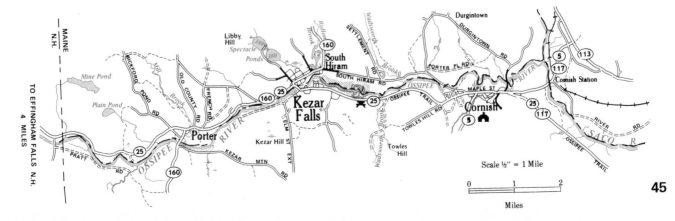

Scale ½" = 1 Mile

0   1   2

Miles

Penobscot River

Overview

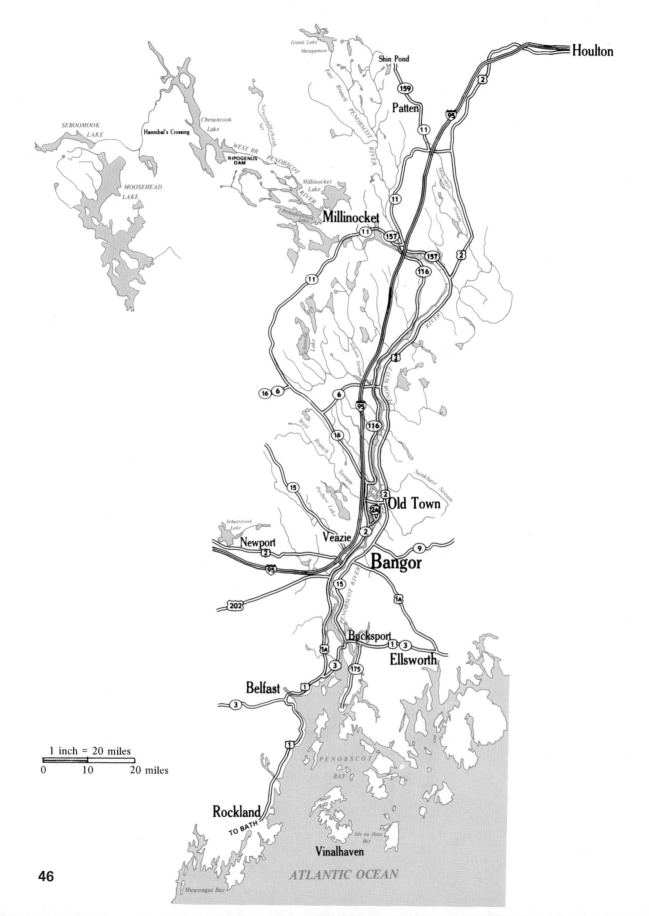

1 inch = 20 miles

0   10   20 miles

Penobscot River
Costigan Area

Penobscot County
Maine Atlas map 33

This is an area of flat water which flows through flat country but has excellent fishing for smallmouth bass. The multitude of islands in the river add to the scenic attraction of the area. The fishing is good all during the warm weather months but the best action comes in June when the bass are spawning.

The fish weigh in the 1½ to 3 pound range. Most of the locals cast plugs or popping bugs to the shorelines but it is possible to troll for them.

This river section is best fished out of a canoe or a motor boat. Hand carried craft can be launched from any of a number of pull-outs which are located on the west side of Route 2. General access to the area is by taking Route 2 north from Bangor.

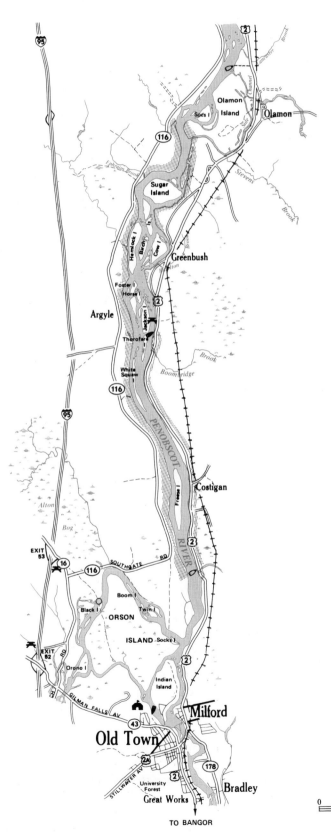

Scale ½″ = 1 Mile

0   1   2

Miles

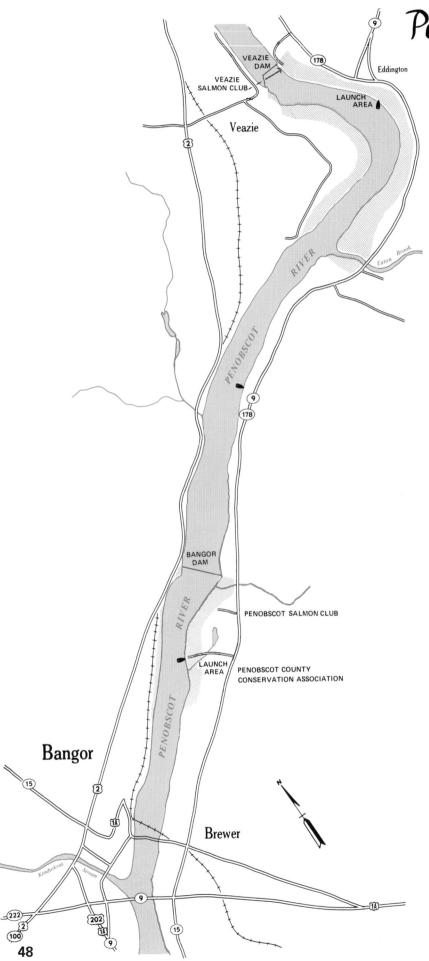

Penobscot River
Veazie to Bangor

Penobscot County
Maine Atlas map 23

The stretch of the Penobscot below the Veazie Dam to Bangor is
the best producer of Atlantic salmon in the state and has the reputa-
tion and crowds of anglers to prove
it.

Best fishing is during the first
two weeks of June, although fish
are taking flies from opening day
well into July and again in September. The best time to fish is during
the first two hours into an ebb tide.
Fishing here is both by wading and
from anchored boats. There is a
public boat launch at the Penobscot County Conservation Associa-
tion club grounds in Brewer off
Route 9. Most of the shore fishing is done from the Brewer side
of the river, starting at the dam and
going well down past the clubhouse
into obvious flat water. There are
also a couple of lies above (within
75 yards of) the old dam, on the
Brewer side.

Fishing is good downstream
from the Veazie Dam to the mouth
of Eaton Brook. There is a boat
launch area at the pipeline right-of-
way on Route 178 about 50 feet
from where the road turns off
Route 9 at Eddington. Access to
Veazie Dam itself is by a dirt road
located in a pine grove leading off
Route 178. The road is about a
quarter mile long and is passable by
high pickup trucks but not passenger cars.

Anglers fish from the Veazie
Dam down on both sides of the
river from shore, wading and using
canoes and boats. Most fish with
floating lines and large flies, up to
5/0 in the spring.

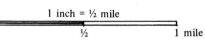

1 inch = ½ mile

0   ½   1 mile

Penobscot River, East Branch
Mattagamon Lake to Seboeis River

Penobscot County
Maine Atlas map 51

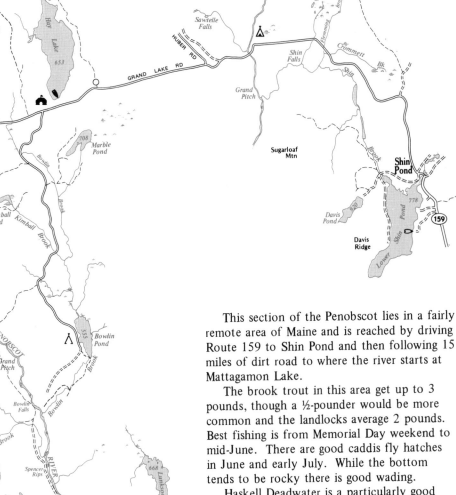

This section of the Penobscot lies in a fairly remote area of Maine and is reached by driving Route 159 to Shin Pond and then following 15 miles of dirt road to where the river starts at Mattagamon Lake.

The brook trout in this area get up to 3 pounds, though a ½-pounder would be more common and the landlocks average 2 pounds. Best fishing is from Memorial Day weekend to mid-June. There are good caddis fly hatches in June and early July. While the bottom tends to be rocky there is good wading.

Haskell Deadwater is a particularly good spot for brook trout and it is most easily reached by taking a conoe down. There is a good campground where the road meets the river. It is possible to follow the west side of the river on a rough, four-wheel drive quality road. This is a big woods area which offers good views of Mount Katahdin in the distance and lots of moose.

Scale ½" = 1 Mile

0   1   2

Miles

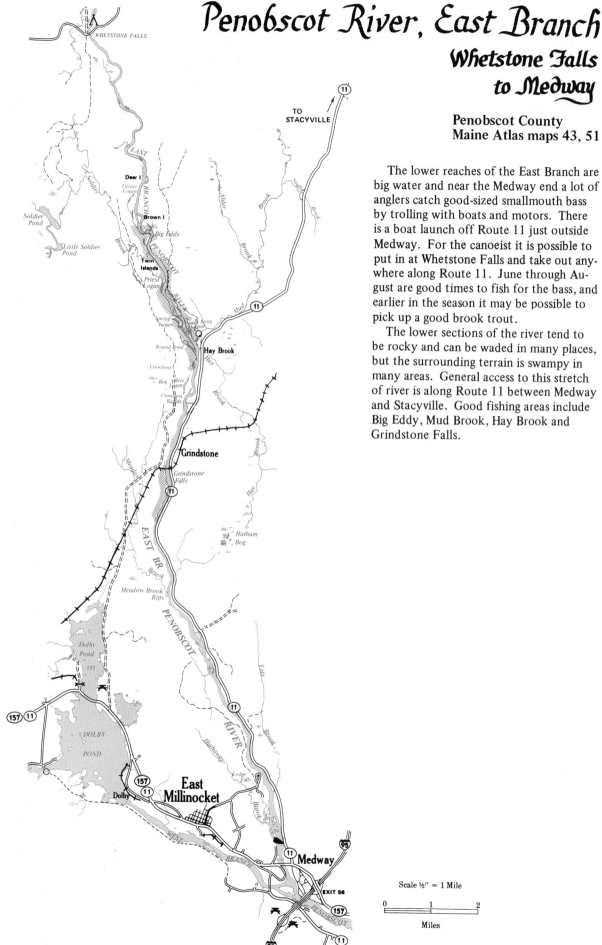

Penobscot River, East Branch
Whetstone Falls to Medway

Penobscot County
Maine Atlas maps 43, 51

The lower reaches of the East Branch are big water and near the Medway end a lot of anglers catch good-sized smallmouth bass by trolling with boats and motors. There is a boat launch off Route 11 just outside Medway. For the canoeist it is possible to put in at Whetstone Falls and take out anywhere along Route 11. June through August are good times to fish for the bass, and earlier in the season it may be possible to pick up a good brook trout.

The lower sections of the river tend to be rocky and can be waded in many places, but the surrounding terrain is swampy in many areas. General access to this stretch of river is along Route 11 between Medway and Stacyville. Good fishing areas include Big Eddy, Mud Brook, Hay Brook and Grindstone Falls.

Scale ½″ = 1 Mile

0   1   2

Miles

Penobscot River, West Branch
Seboomook Lake to Hannibal's Crossing

Piscataquis and Somerset Counties
Maine Atlas map 49

The West Branch leaves Seboomook Lake and flows in a crest above the top of Moosehead Lake before turning north to join Chesuncook Lake. The stretch of river from Seboomook Dam to Hannibal's Crossing is a good producer of landlocked salmon which average 2 pounds and sometimes make it to 5 pounds.

The best fishing is in the slick water just below Seboomook Dam during June and July. Fly fishermen will do well to fish with nymphs and wooly worms in yellow and green hues and in sizes 6 and 8.

Fishing is possible from the shore. Wading conditions are good on a rocky bottom although some may find it convenient to fish from midstream in an anchored canoe.

Reach this area by taking the Great Northern Paper Company Road out of Rockwood to the 20 mile check point and turning right. These roads are rough. There are campsites, lean-tos and a store at Seboomook Landing and state campsites at the dam.

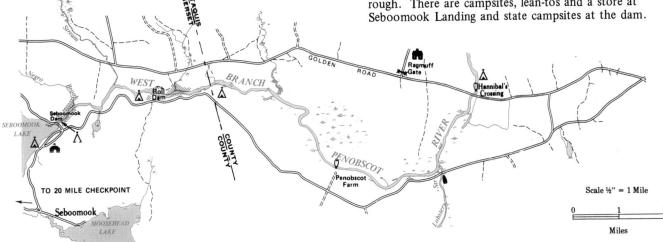

Ripogenus Dam to Little Ambejackmockamus Falls

Piscataquis County
Maine Atlas map 50

Some people call the West Branch below Ripogenus Dam the best landlocked salmon river in the country. It may well be, and it has also got to be one of the most intensely fished as well. The water here has just come out of the bottom of Ripogenus Dam and is cool throughout the year, even during summer drought. However, June is probably the best time to fish here.

This is big, heavy water. While there is fishing from the shores and some places to wade, a canoe is a good idea for reaching the best water such as the middle portions of the Big Eddy.

The river is bordered by roads and trails on both sides. There is a camping area right at Big Eddy. The salmon in this area sometimes get to 7 or 8 pounds, but 2-pounders are more common. An occasional brook trout will also be taken.

Access to the area is by taking the Baxter State Park Road out of Millinocket and then traveling the Golden Road.

Scale ½″ = 1 Mile

0   1   2

Miles

Penobscot River, West Branch
Nesowadnehunk Deadwater

Piscataquis County
Maine Atlas map 50

The Nesowadnehunk Deadwater, which lies between Big Ambejackmockamus and Nesowadnehunk Falls, is one of the best opening day fishing spots in the northern half of the state. While they may have to brave snow flurries, anglers often take 3 and 4 pound landlocked salmon here as the season gets underway.

The deadwater is accessible by driving the Baxter State Park Road out of Millinocket. The huge deadwater, looking like a long, narrow lake, is plainly visible from the road. Just before crossing Horserace Brook there is a dirt road leading into a large gravel pit where there is a good launch area that can handle a fairly big boat and motor. Trolling is the normal method of fishing this stretch of the river and fish can be caught right through the summer, although August is not a productive time.

The scenic value of this area is very high with Sentinel Mountain etched against the sky across the river. This is also a prime area for spotting bald eagles. You can camp in the gravel pit, but expect plenty of company as this is a heavily fished area.

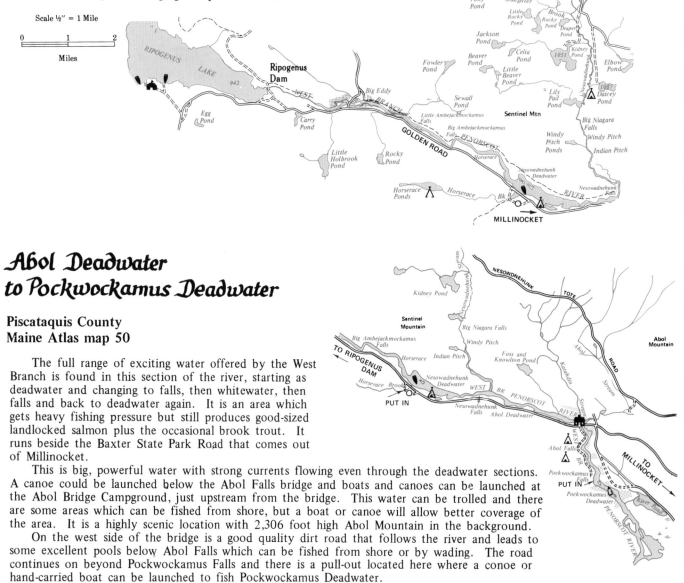

Abol Deadwater
to Pockwockamus Deadwater

Piscataquis County
Maine Atlas map 50

The full range of exciting water offered by the West Branch is found in this section of the river, starting as deadwater and changing to falls, then whitewater, then falls and back to deadwater again. It is an area which gets heavy fishing pressure but still produces good-sized landlocked salmon plus the occasional brook trout. It runs beside the Baxter State Park Road that comes out of Millinocket.

This is big, powerful water with strong currents flowing even through the deadwater sections. A canoe could be launched below the Abol Falls bridge and boats and canoes can be launched at the Abol Bridge Campground, just upstream from the bridge. This water can be trolled and there are some areas which can be fished from shore, but a boat or canoe will allow better coverage of the area. It is a highly scenic location with 2,306 foot high Abol Mountain in the background.

On the west side of the bridge is a good quality dirt road that follows the river and leads to some excellent pools below Abol Falls which can be fished from shore or by wading. The road continues on beyond Pockwockamus Falls and there is a pull-out located here where a canoe or hand-carried boat can be launched to fish Pockwockamus Deadwater.

June is the prime fishing month here, but there is plenty of water to hold fish during all the open water fishing months.

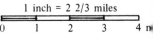

Piscataqua River

Kittery & Portsmouth, N.H.

York County, Maine and
Rockingham County, N.H.
map 1

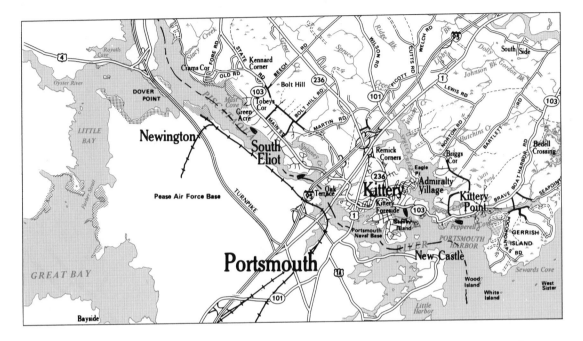

Scale ½″ = 1 Mile

0   1   2

Miles

OVERVIEW
See next two pages
for detail

There is considerable fishing attention being paid to this border river because of a Coho salmon stocking program instituted by New Hampshire. These salmon, native to the West Coast, are released as smolts and come back in the summer and fall as adults which often exceed 10 pounds. Best time to fish in the Kittery-Portsmouth area is from July to September with good fishing in the New Hampshire tributaries into November.

There are numerous handy launching areas. Small boats and canoes can be put in near Kittery Yacht Club on Pepperell Cove. This is a fishing hotspot and the time to try is several hours before and after high tide. Most catches are taken on mackerel strips drifted from anchored boats. Trolling is routine and fly fishing and casting are possible.

Another launch is adjacent to Kittery Grammar School, just off Route 1 and east of the Navy Yard entrance. Fishing is good here in late August and September on both rising and falling tides. This is a good canoe area but there are fast tidal rips near the bridge to the Navy Yard. Try casting flies and spinning lures.

The Eliot shore has a public launch. Fish upstream to the mouth of Salmon Falls River. This is a good trolling area or you can anchor and cast in rips and below rocks and bars.

On the New Hampshire side, there is a ramp at Hilton State Park off Route 16 that is good for all tides except for larger outboards at low water. Fish in Little Bay upstream of the bridges to Oyster River and Adams Point. Best times are late September and October.

Caution: tidal currents can be immensely strong and small boats and canoes must stay out of the main channels, especially on outgoing tides.

Note: Anyone fishing on the New Hampshire side of the river will need a New Hampshire fishing license, but no license is required for tidal waters in Maine.

Pleasant River
Saco Falls to Columbia Falls

Washington County
Maine Atlas map 25

The Pleasant River may be the sleeper among Maine's Atlantic salmon rivers. The local anglers tell visitors it is not a good place to catch salmon, but they keep right on fishing it themselves.

There are good salmon lies below Saco Falls and most of the best fishing is from there to Columbia Falls. There are good pools at the North Branch and Little River. Right behind the old school house in Columbia Falls and at the mouth of Little River are the best spring salmon fishing spots during the first week of May.

The best overall time to fish the Pleasant for salmon is during the four weeks after Memorial Day and again in September. Most people fish from the banks or from a canoe.

There is excellent trout fishing to be had during May and early June by putting in at Pleasant River Lake and canoeing downstream to any of the crossing roads.

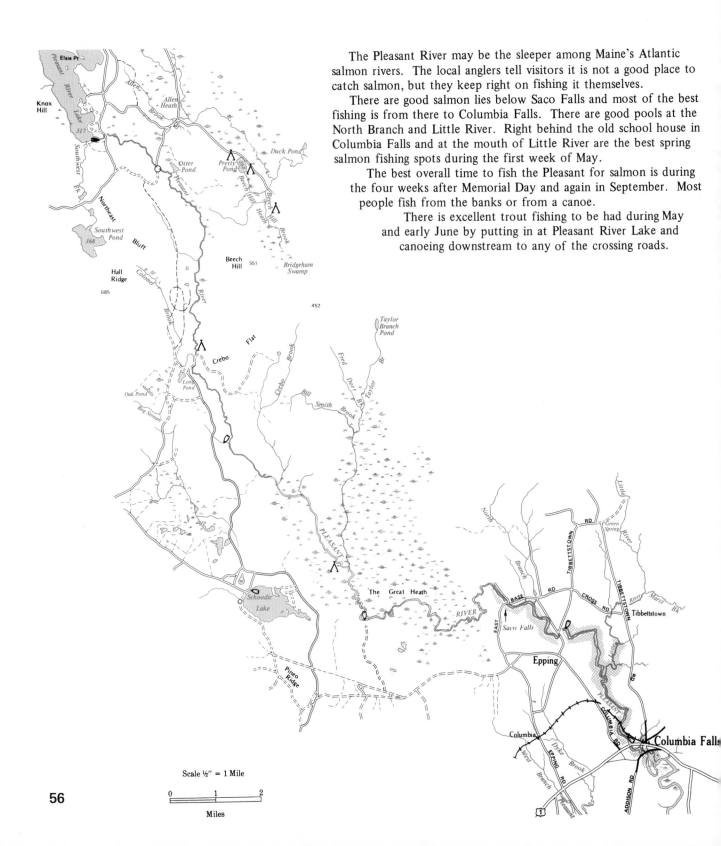

Scale ½" = 1 Mile

0   1   2
Miles

Presque Isle Stream
T 10 R3 to Presque Isle

Aroostook County
Maine Atlas maps 58, 64, 65

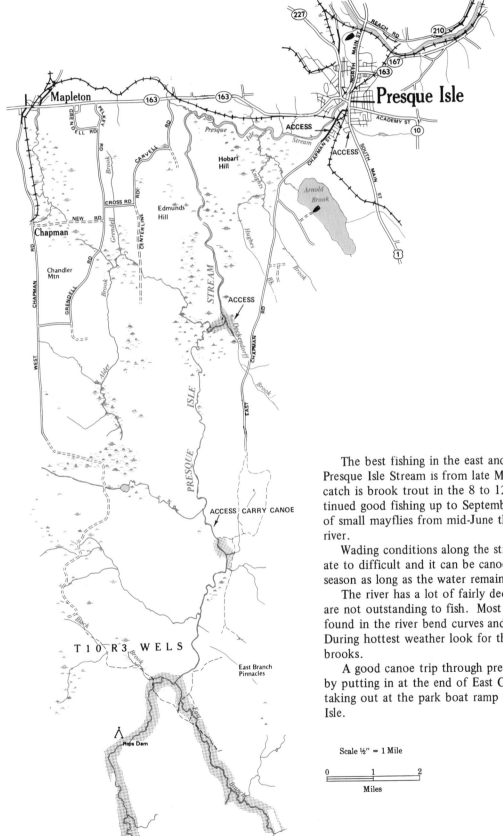

The best fishing in the east and west tributaries of Presque Isle Stream is from late May to early June. The catch is brook trout in the 8 to 12 inch range with continued good fishing up to September. There are hatches of small mayflies from mid-June through July on the river.

Wading conditions along the stream vary from moderate to difficult and it can be canoed during the early season as long as the water remains fairly high.

The river has a lot of fairly deep, slow pools which are not outstanding to fish. Most of the trout will be found in the river bend curves and in the riffle areas. During hottest weather look for them at the mouths of brooks.

A good canoe trip through pretty country can be made by putting in at the end of East Chapman Road and taking out at the park boat ramp in the city of Presque Isle.

Scale ½″ = 1 Mile

0   1   2

Miles

Prestile Stream
Easton to Canadian Border

Aroostook County
Maine Atlas maps 59, 65

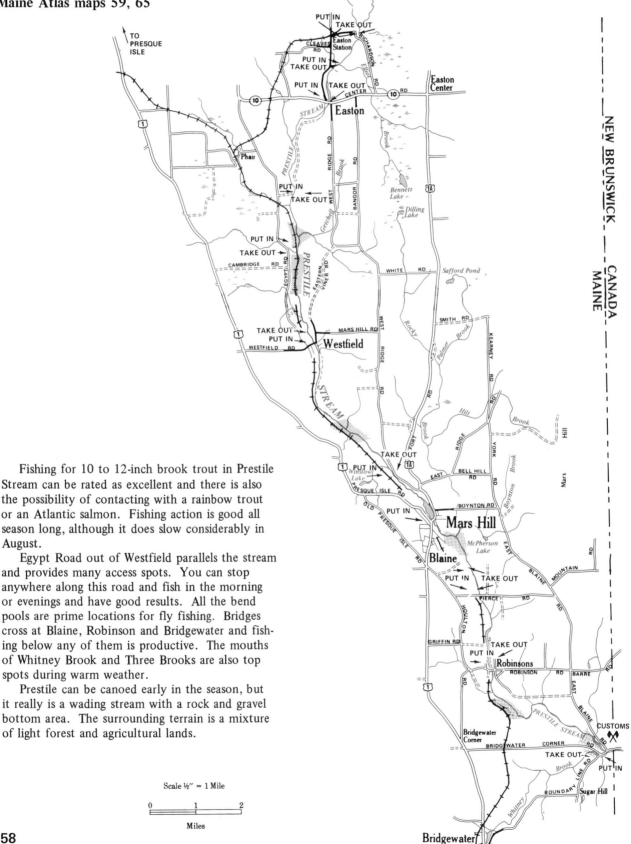

Fishing for 10 to 12-inch brook trout in Prestile Stream can be rated as excellent and there is also the possibility of contacting with a rainbow trout or an Atlantic salmon. Fishing action is good all season long, although it does slow considerably in August.

Egypt Road out of Westfield parallels the stream and provides many access spots. You can stop anywhere along this road and fish in the morning or evenings and have good results. All the bend pools are prime locations for fly fishing. Bridges cross at Blaine, Robinson and Bridgewater and fishing below any of them is productive. The mouths of Whitney Brook and Three Brooks are also top spots during warm weather.

Prestile can be canoed early in the season, but it really is a wading stream with a rock and gravel bottom area. The surrounding terrain is a mixture of light forest and agricultural lands.

Scale ½" = 1 Mile

0   1   2

Miles

Pushaw Stream
Pushaw Lake to Old Town

Penobscot County
Maine Atlas map 33

Pushaw is a good-sized stream that flows through mostly flat and swampy country. General access is by Route 43 out of Old Town.

Canoes and car top boats can be launched on the south side of Route 43 where it crosses the stream east of Pushaw Lake. Upstream is flat weedy water that is ideal pickerel, perch and bass habitat. A boat can be paddled up to the dam at the lake.

Downstream from the launching area are rapids above and below the point where Route 43 crosses. Below that is mostly flatwater to the dam located below Interstate 95.

Scale ½" = 1 Mile

0   1   2

Miles

Rapid River
Lower Richardson Lake to Umbagog Lake

Oxford County
Maine Atlas map 18

This short river is well named because it moves in a hurry on its way downstream, but in between the whitewater stretches are some beautiful and highly productive pools. The principal fishery is for landlocked salmon in the 2 pound class, and there are brook trout as well.

Fishing in the Rapid is good throughout the season, with peaks in June and September. There are some caddis and mayfly hatches. Some places can be waded, but most fishing is done from shore. Many canoes and kayaks have been destroyed on the Rapid.

The mile stretch between Middle Dam and Pond in the River is the most heavily fished, partly because it is the most easily reached. There are excellent pools all along the river close to Umbagog Lake itself. A dirt road follows the north side of the river and the trails to the various pools are well-trodden and easy to spot.

Usual access to the Rapid is by taking Route 120 out of Rumford and turning onto the South Arm road at Andover. There is a campground and launching site at South Arm, on Lower Richardson Lake. The lake must be crossed for 5 miles to reach Middle Dam.

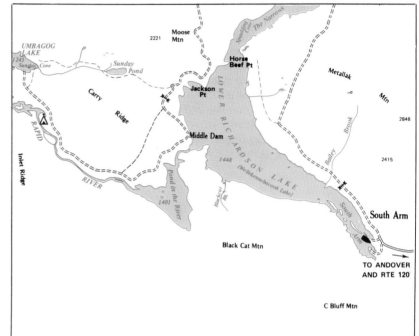

OVERVIEW
See Detail Below

Scale ½″ = 1 Mile

0   1   2

Miles

1 inch = 1 mile

0   ½   1 mile

Roach River
First Roach Pond to Moosehead Lake

Piscataquis County
Maine Atlas map 41

Roach River can be most easily reached by following the road leading out of Greenville on the east side of Moosehead Lake, which goes past Lily Bay State Park.

Landlocked salmon in the 3 to 4-pound class are the prime attraction of the Roach River, but there are some jumbo trout available as well.

Most people do their fishing just below the dam at First Roach Pond. However, there is a dirt road on the north side of the river just beyond the old hotel. Access may prove a problem here, but inquire at the nearby Kokadjo store. There is a series of excellent pools located about 1/8-mile downstream and chest waders will prove helpful for fishing them.

There is another excellent pool formed where the river flows into Moosehead Lake. This pool is an excellent place for wading and fly casting and holds good fish. There are also several pools upstream from this point. You can reach this part of the river by following the dirt road which crosses Lazy Tom Stream and walking down Jewett Brook to the river, but a much better method is to launch a boat at Jewett Cove and cross Moosehead Lake to the river mouth. The middle portions of the river are not worth bothering with as there is very little holding water. Best times to fish the Roach are in June and September although the river holds fish throughout the season.

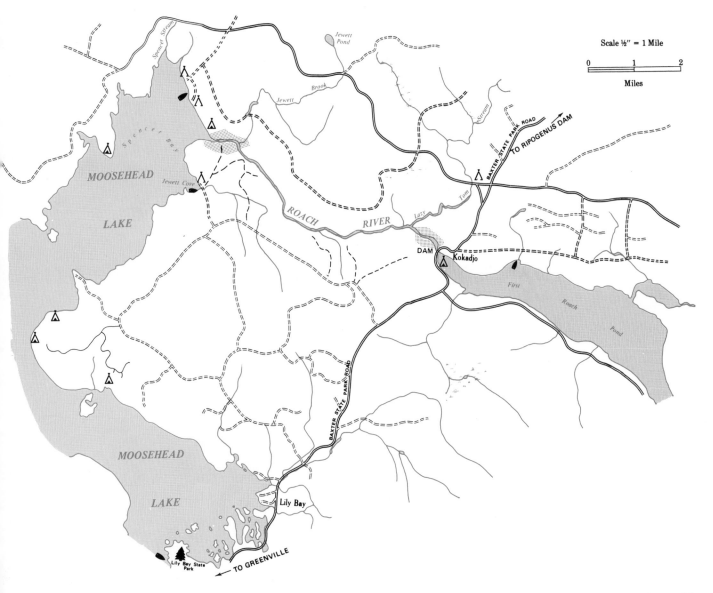

Royal River
Yarmouth

**Cumberland County
Maine Atlas map 5**

The Royal River in Yarmouth offers one of the two sea-run brown trout fisheries in Maine now being supported by annual stockings. While fish can be caught almost any time of year in this suburban setting, the true runs of browns take place in October and November. They average 2 pounds, but there are a number of fish above the 5 pound mark as well.

The best fishing is from East Elm Street to the Interstate 95 overpass below high tide level.

1   marks the newest fish ladder. About 100 yards upstream from this ladder is a good hard boat launch and parking for upstream fishing. The river can be navigated as far upstream as the Route 9 bridge. While there are some trout upstream, it is mostly bass and pickerel water.

2   is the location of a new paved pathway which runs from East Elm to Bridge Street.

3   is the site of the lower fishway.

4   marks the most popular fishing from Bridge Street and below.

5   is the low falls and location of productive fishing.

6   is the location of an all-tide boat launch providing access to salt water.

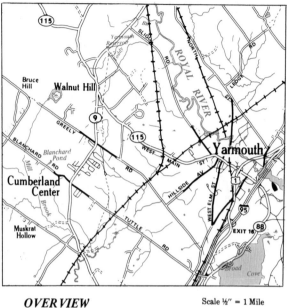

**OVERVIEW
See Detail Below**

Scale ½″ = 1 Mile

0   1   2

Miles

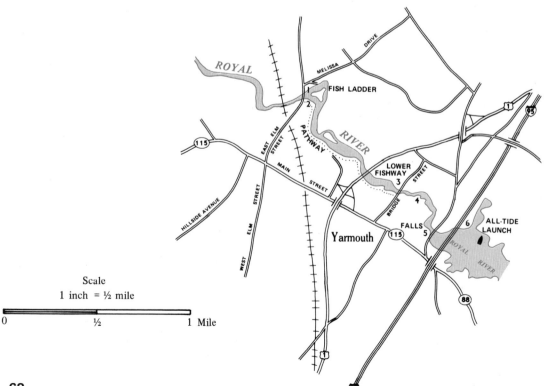

Scale
1 inch = ½ mile

0   ½   1 Mile

Saco River
Hiram Falls to Limington Rip

Cumberland, York and Oxford Counties
Maine Atlas map 4

This section of the Saco is probably the most productive portion for brown trout fishing, with many 8 to 10-inch stocked fish taken, but some much larger hold-over fish being caught as well. Hiram Falls and Limington Rip are both good producing areas. The falls and whitewater areas around Steep Falls also are productive.

Best fishing time is in late May and June and again in September. There are sections of this river which can be waded but it is one of the most popular canoeing areas in the state.

The stretch from Hiram Falls to Limington makes a good two-day canoe and fishing trip and is about 15 miles long. Canoes can be put in at Hiram Falls to the left of the power station off Route 117. Some of the rips should be scouted before they are run on this river. Steep Falls must be portaged on the left shore about 100 yards above the bridge. Limington Rip is another piece of heavy water which the average canoeist may want to portage around.

This section of the Saco is located to the west of Sebago Lake and is best reached by taking Route 25 west from Gorham and turning right onto Route 113 west of Standish.

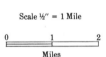

Scale ½" = 1 Mile

0   1   2
Miles

Pepperell Dam to Atlantic Ocean

York County
Maine Atlas map 3

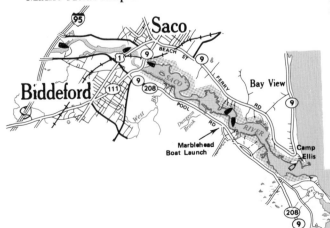

Tidal portions of the Saco River have had pollution problems in the past from industrial wastes coming from manufacturing plants in the twin towns of Biddeford and Saco, but conditions are generally much cleaner today.

Boat access is from the Marblehead Boat Launch off Route 208 in Biddeford and the Camp Ellis Boat Ramp off Route 9. Both are solid ramps capable of handling large craft. The river is navigable up to Pepperell Dam between Biddeford and Saco. Atlantic salmon are now being stocked and caught in this section of the river.

The lower Saco is best known for its striped bass fishing, both in the river and at its mouth, as well as in nearby Biddeford Pool. Most of these fish are schoolies in the 2 to 5 pound range. Bluefish and mackerel also enter the river at times.

Scale ½" = 1 Mile

0   1   2
Miles

63

St. Croix Stream
St. Croix Lake to Masardis

**Aroostook County
Maine Atlas map 58**

Scale ½" = 1 Mile

0   1   2

Miles

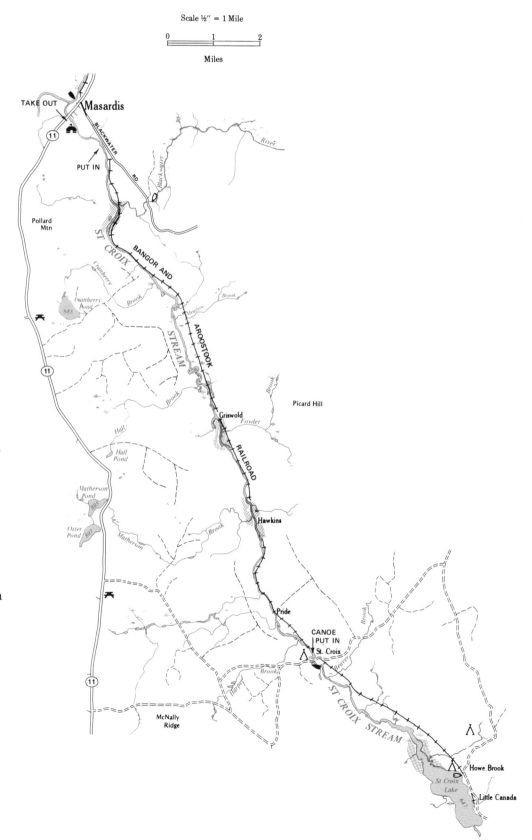

St. Croix Stream of-
fers good spring fishing
for brook trout in the
8 to 10-inch class al-
though fish to 14 inches
are not uncommon.
The stream can be ca-
noed during the high
water of spring from
the lake to Masardis
Landing.

The stream is closely
followed by the Bangor
and Aroostook Railroad
tracks and flows through
spruce-fir forest. The
best pools are at the
junctions of Blackwater
River, Fowler Brook
and Matherson Brook.
The fishing is best from
late May to mid-June
and mayfly hatches
occur in June. The
river can be waded on
a bottom of rocks and
boulders interspersed
with gravel.

St. John River
Fourth St. John Pond to Allagash Village

Somerset, Aroostook and Piscataquis Counties
Maine Atlas maps 48, 54, 60, 61, 66, 70

The 132 mile stretch of the St. John River between Fourth St. John Pond and Allagash Village is one of Maine's two major canoe attractions, the second being the Allagash Wilderness Waterway.

Wilderness trips on the St. John can be arranged to encompass any length of time by varying the length of the river travelled. Generally trips are broken down as follows: Fourth St. John Pond to Baker Lake. Baker Lake to American Realty Road. Nine Mile Bridge to Seven Islands. Seven Islands to Big Black River, and Big Black River to Allagash. Depending on the water level (which is subject to fluctuations up to 2 feet within a

For U.S. customs hours in Northwestern Maine, call (207) 668-3711

12 hour period after heavy rain), canoeists move down the river at speeds from 12 miles an hour to ½ mile per hour.

Brook trout are the main attraction throughout the river and most of them are in the 6 to 10 inch category although much larger fish are taken. They can be found almost anyplace in the river during late May and early June and particularly in the good pools. Later in the season look for them around the cool mouths of feeder streams. There are good June insect hatches on the river.

Anyone considering fishing the St. John, or making a canoe trip down it, should obtain a copy of DeLorme's Allagash and St. John Guide, which, besides being the most detailed map of the region available, also contains a wealth of information on the various trips which can be made down the river.

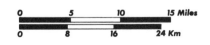

Sandy River
Phillips to Farmington

Franklin County
Maine Atlas maps 19, 20

The Sandy River is one of the most idyllic rivers to wade and fly fish in the state. The only trouble is that the fishery is definitely an up and down proposition.

The Sandy is stocked with brown trout and also has wild brook trout, but it is a heavy run-off river surrounded by steep mountains. The river suffers from anchor ice, flooding and scouring during bad springs which can throw the fishing off for years at a time.

On the other hand, from June well into July it has water cool enough to hold fish and good hatches of both mayflies and caddis flies. Best fishing is in the evening. If the browns have been recently stocked they will be in the 6 to 8-inch class. Holdovers will be in the 10 to 14-inch category. The brook trout run 8 to 10-inches.

There is some whitewater in this stretch of the river but it is easily canoeable with the possibility of some dragging at mid-summer levels. There is ample access all along the river with Route 149 offering more spots than Route 4. Access to the river's most notable pool, the Devil's Elbow near Stubbs Mountain, is from Route 4 which passes within a backcast of this stretch of deep water.

Most of the flats near the river are actively farmed and most of the vistas are filled with mountains, making this portion of the Sandy extremely scenic.

Scale ½″ = 1 Mile

Miles

Sandy Stream
Baxter State Park to Millinocket Lake

Penobscot and Piscataquis Counties
Maine Atlas map 51

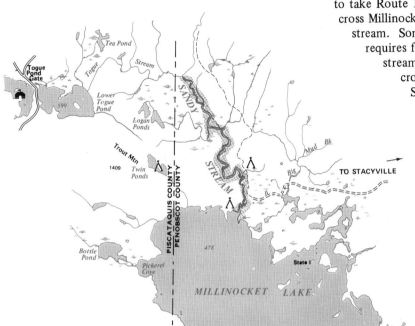

Access to Sandy Stream can be varied. One possibility is to take Route 157 to Millinocket continue north and then cross Millinocket Lake by boat to get to the mouth of the stream. Some anglers travel the Stacyville Road but this requires figuring out the turnoff to the left to reach the stream, which is not marked. Sometimes fishermen cross Togue Pond in the southern part of Baxter State Park by boat and walk down Togue Stream to its junction with Sandy Stream.

The lower end of Sandy Stream is influenced by the lake and landlocked salmon up to 16 inches are taken. There are also landlocks in Togue Stream. The brook trout in the stream range from 6 to 12 inches.

Wading in Sandy Stream is easy with a sandy, gravelly bottom. Fishing is good in June and July and there are some insect hatches.

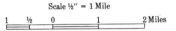

Scale ½″ = 1 Mile

1   ½   0   1   2 Miles

Sebasticook River
Benton to Winslow

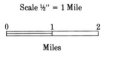

Scale ½″ = 1 Mile

0   1   2

Miles

Kennebec County
Maine Atlas map 21

The lower reaches of the Sebasticook River flow through mostly flat countryside of mixed woods and farmland. The river is backed up all the way to Benton Falls by a dam at Winslow and is flat water.

Access for canoes can be made by following the Garland Road out of Winslow and launching in the grassy area just above the Winslow dam by following the road which goes behind LaVerdiere's Drugstore just off Route 201, in Winslow. The stream is only suitable for small craft.

The river from Benton Falls down for a couple of miles offers the best fishing for smallmouth bass up to 4 pounds, pickerel up to 3 pounds and excellent white perch. An occasional landlocked salmon is caught at Benton Falls and a wide variety of fish show up just below the dam in Winslow which is a good place to try any time of the year. This section of the river will produce fish during all the summer months, but in hot weather it should be fished early or late in the day.

The river bottom is mostly mud and the edges are weed and lily pad covered so you must either fish from the banks or use a small boat.

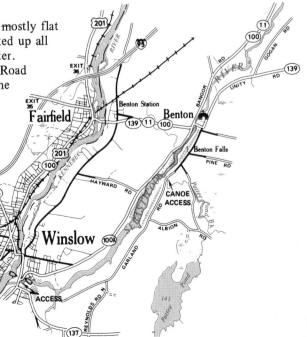

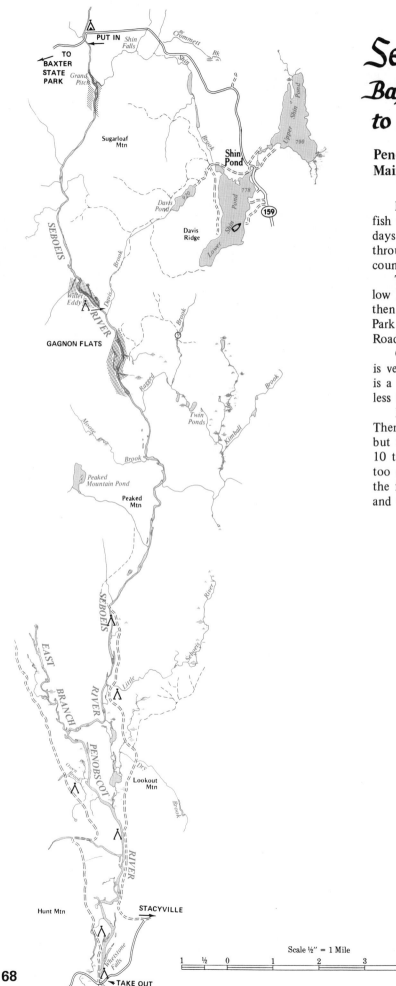

Seboeis River
Baxter State Park Road to Stacyville

Penobscot County
Maine Atlas map 51

It takes at least a two-day canoe trip to fish this stretch of the Seboeis River, but four days would be even better as the trip leads through some of the most attractive mountain country in Maine.

To reach the upper end of the river, follow Route 159 from Patten to Shin Pond and then take the road leading to Baxter State Park. Take out is at the Sherman Lumber Road in Stacyville.

Grand Pitch near the beginning of the trip is very dangerous as it comes up suddenly and is a 25-foot falls. Portage around the falls is less than ¼-mile.

Best fishing is from May 15 to July 4. There is an occasional salmon in the river, but the main attraction is brook trout in the 10 to 18-inch category. Much of the river is too deep for good wading. Best spots to try the fishing are below Grand Pitch, Willet Eddy and Gagnon Flats.

Scale ½″ = 1 Mile

1   ½   0   1   2   3   4   5 Miles

Sheepscot River
Sheepscot Pond to Long Pond

Knox, Kennebec, Lincoln and Waldo Counties
Maine Atlas map 13

While it has the name of a river, the Sheepscot in this area is little more than a large brook. However, it flows cold through the summer months and holds brown trout, brook trout and landlocked salmon. Most of the salmon are sub-legal size but the trout are often in the 8 to 12-inch range.

Best time to fish is the month of June when there are extremely heavy mayfly hatches. The river is heavily grown over and casting of any kind is difficult. An exception is at the fish hatchery near Sheepscot Pond. The river flows under a bridge here and it forms a pool which is heavily fished. Best fishing is downstream from here. Look for a dirt road leading off the main road for access. The river gets wilder, swampier and more difficult to walk as it nears Route 105 in Somerville, but this section also offers the best fishing. The area just above and below James Pond is a deadwater.

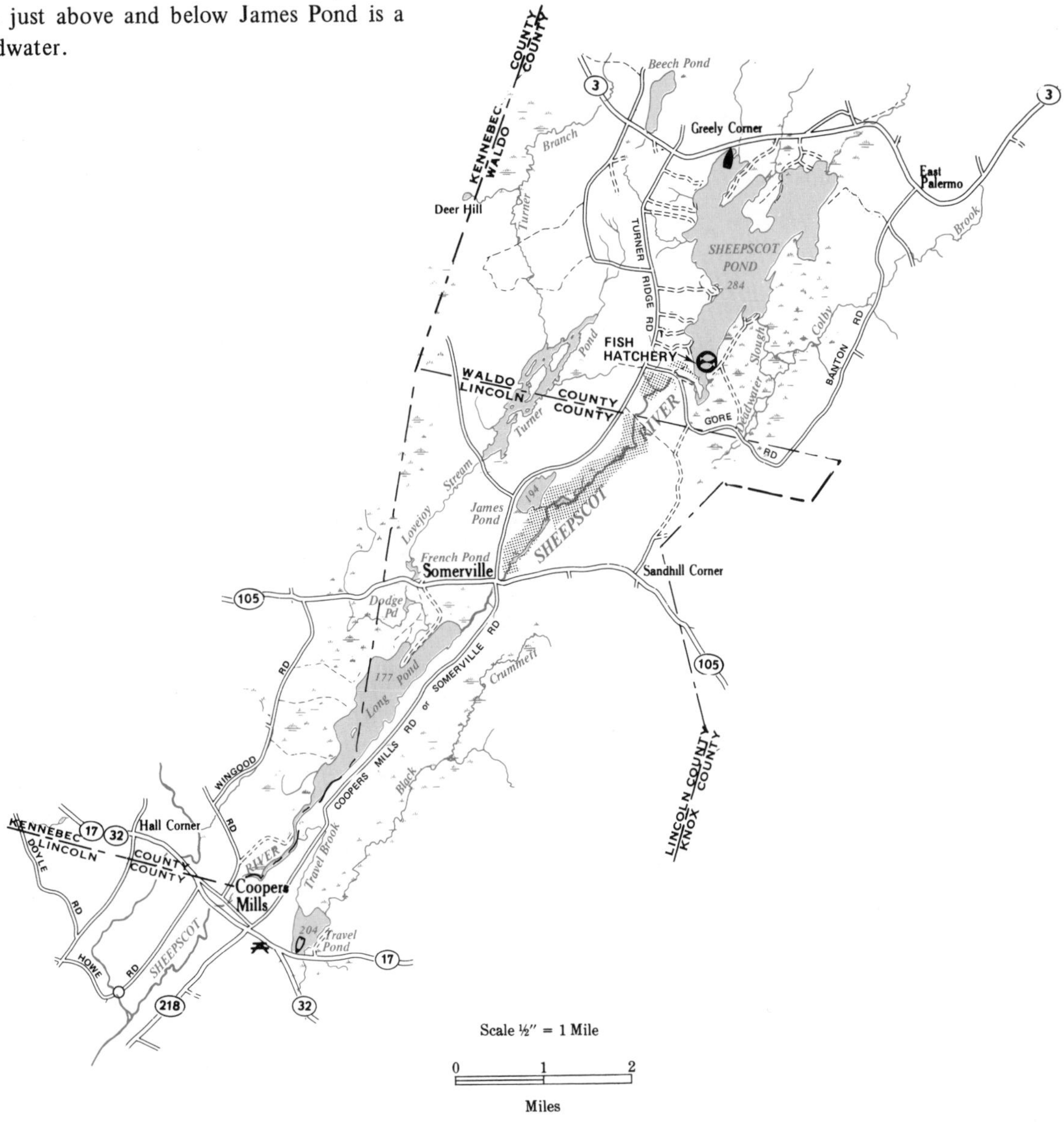

Scale ½" = 1 Mile

0 1 2

Miles

Sheepscot River
North Whitefield to Headtide Dam

Lincoln County
Maine Atlas map 13

The Sheepscot River flows through a mixture of woods and farmland in this section, a
favorite with canoeists, especially in May and
April when the river runs high. Put-in is at
Route 126 in North Whitefield and take out is
at Head Tide Dam. This section can be canoed
in June if water levels remain fairly high.

There are wild brook trout and wild brown
trout in this section and the best fishing is
from mid-May to mid-June when there will be
good caddis and mayfly hatches.

There are brook trout in North Whitefield
in the fast water above the bridge down to
slow water. Brook and brown trout can be
taken in the vicinity of Route 194 and there
are browns in the first set of pools above
Head Tide Dam.

The bottom tends to be very slippery in
this stretch of water but a pair of chest waders
comes in handy for fishing some of the larger
pools where smallmouth bass can also be
caught.

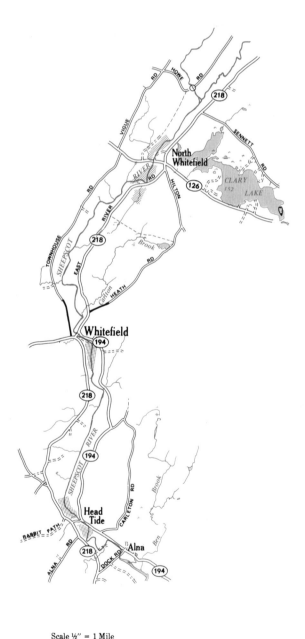

Scale ½″ = 1 Mile

0   1   2

Miles

Head Tide Dam to Reversing Falls

Lincoln County
Maine Atlas maps 7,13

This section of the Sheepscot is outstanding because of a natural reversing falls and the presence of Atlantic salmon.

The reversing falls is located where two points of land nearly meet about one-eighth mile below the bridge in Sheepscot. Access to the area is over the King's Highway road or by walking along the east shore from the bridge. Most of the fishing is done from the south shore to the upstream edge of the falls where salmon lies are located and it is done during the last half of a falling tide and the first half of a rising tide. Other known salmon lies are below the Alna Bridge and in several bend pools upstream from that point, as well as below the Head Tide Dam and the first upstream bend pool above the dam.

In late May there is the possibility of catching a sea-run brown trout in any of these pools and during July and August striped bass and mackerel are sometimes caught in the area below Reversing Falls. The salmon fishing is good in June and better in September, although the annual catch of Atlantic salmon from the Sheepscot is always a small number.

Access is by Route 218 out of Wiscasset.

1 inch = 1¾ miles

0   1   2 miles

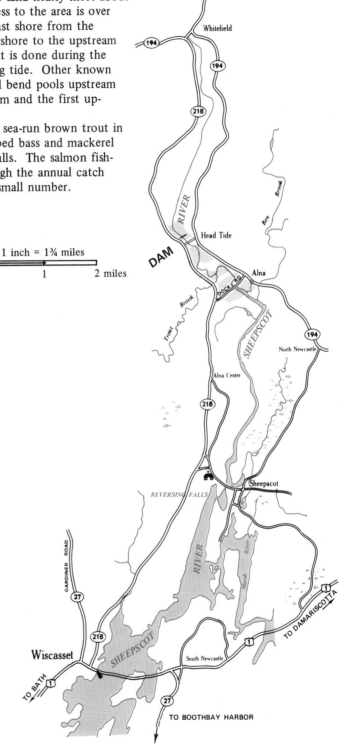

Sheepscot River
Wiscasset to Atlantic Ocean

Lincoln and Sagadahoc Counties
Maine Atlas map 7

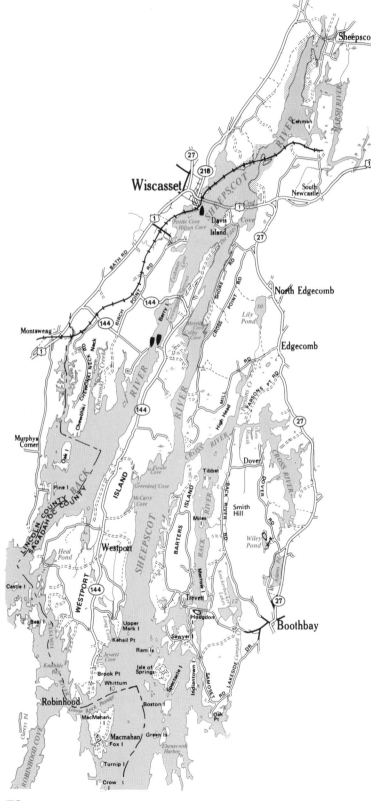

The public boat launch in Wiscasset can be found by following the first street before the bridge on the south side of Route 1.

This portion of the Sheepscot is typical of many Maine tidal estuaries in being a large body of water that is well protected from waves and wind. In the summer even a small boat can handle this water, although the heavy tidal currents would prove too much for a canoe.

Mackerel are probably the prime attraction here and many people fish from the Route 1 bridge to catch them. There are also stripers in this water and flounder can be found in sandy bottom areas. At times immense schools of poggies run up this estuary as do Atlantic salmon and an occasional coho salmon.

A good fishing trip for trolling can be made by traveling down the Sheepscot to the end of Westport Island and coming back up the Back River.

Best fishing here is in July and August.

Scale ½″ = 1 Mile

1   ½   0   1   2   3   4   5 Miles

Sunkhaze Stream
Milford

Penobscot County
Maine Atlas map 33

Sunkhaze Stream has good to excellent fishing for brook trout in the 6 to 10-inch size range. Best fishing is in May and June when there are good hatches of caddis and mayflies.

The upper sections of the stream can be waded on a sandy and gravelly bottom. Near Route 2 the stream is too deep to wade. There is a canoe access where the stream crosses Route 2.

The County Road out of Milford provides access to the upper parts of the stream which is also where the best fishing is located.

All the fish in Sunkhaze Stream are wild as there is no stocking and the fishing is subject to good and bad years as a result.

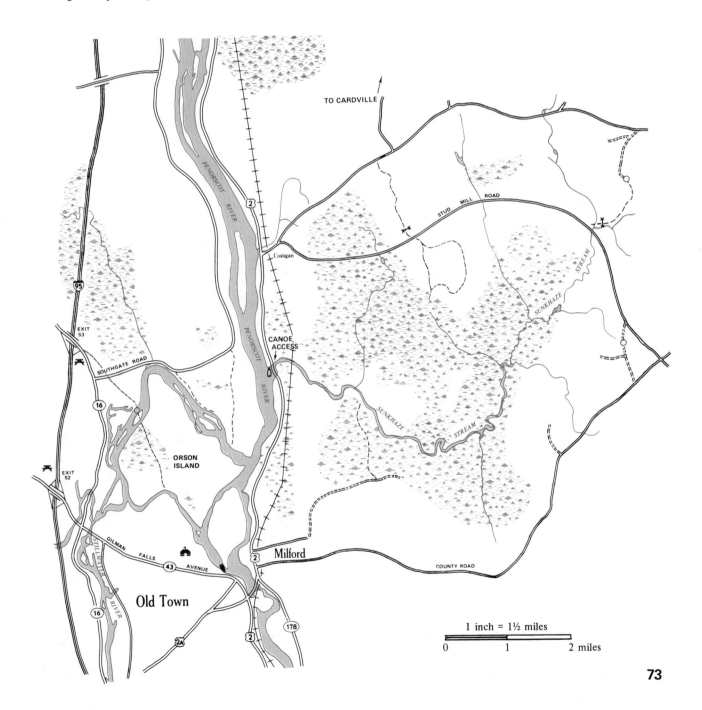

1 inch = 1½ miles

0   1   2 miles

Trout Brook
Black Brook Farm to Grand Lake Mattagamon

Piscataquis and Penobscot Counties
Maine Atlas maps 50, 51, 57

Trout Brook is a very clear, cold brook which crosses a large part of northern Baxter State Park before flowing into Grand Lake Mattagamon. It is a very cold stream and is best fished in July and August for trout in the 6 to 12-inch range.

This is a highly attractive stream with many large, shallow pools which make for good wading. There are mountains in almost every skyline along the way and plenty of wildlife in the area as added interest. A good road follows the stream, making access easy.

You can get to Trout Brook by entering the Park at the southern entrance but a more direct route would be to take Route 159 to Shin Pond and then follow the road to Baxter Park.

Morrell
Pond

Hay
Brook
Logan

Norway Dam

PENOBSCOT COUNTY
PISCATAQUIS COUNTY

Mountain Catcher
Pond

Second
Lake

GRAND   LAKE
654

Big
Logan

First
Lake
654

Lousie
Island

Hub Hill
Cove

MATTAGAMON LAKE
(Grand Lake)

Birch Pt

Boody Bk

TROUT   BROOK   Trout Brook

Trout Brook Mtn

Mattagamon
Gate

Horse Mtn

TROUT

Wadleigh Mtn

Littlefield
Pond

High Pond
926

Billfish

Wadleigh
Brook

Fowler
Green

Dry
Brook

Fowler

Lower
Fowler Pond   862

Long Pond

Billfish Mtn

Trout Bk

Pond Bk

Brook

Middle
Fowler Pond

TO RTE 159
AND
SHIN POND

BROOK

Gifford Brook

Little Peaked
Mtn

Barrell Ridge

Big Peaked
Mtn

Black
Bk
Brook

Kennedy

BLACK BROOK FARM

Lower
South
Branch
Pond   981

TROUT

Burnt
Mtn

Black Brook Mtns

Squirt Dam
Mtn

Scale ½" = 1 Mile

0   1   2

Miles

74

Union River

Ellsworth

Hancock County
Maine Atlas map 24

The in-town portion of the Union River in Ellsworth is notable only because there is a small run of Atlantic salmon present.

Anglers at the Union River must contend with a number of obstacles. Water flow is controlled by a hydro-electric dam and is generally too high or too low to make for good fishing conditions and at times the water coming out of the dam is muddy.

Anyone lucky enough to hook a fish in the short fishable piece of river has to work to keep the fish within the confines of the pools just below the dam because if the fish goes through the gorge below that it is usually lost.

Take Route 1 to get to Ellsworth. Going north, you would turn north on the street just after you cross the bridge. Best time to fish the Union River here is in June.

1 inch = ¼ mile

0   ¼   ½ mile

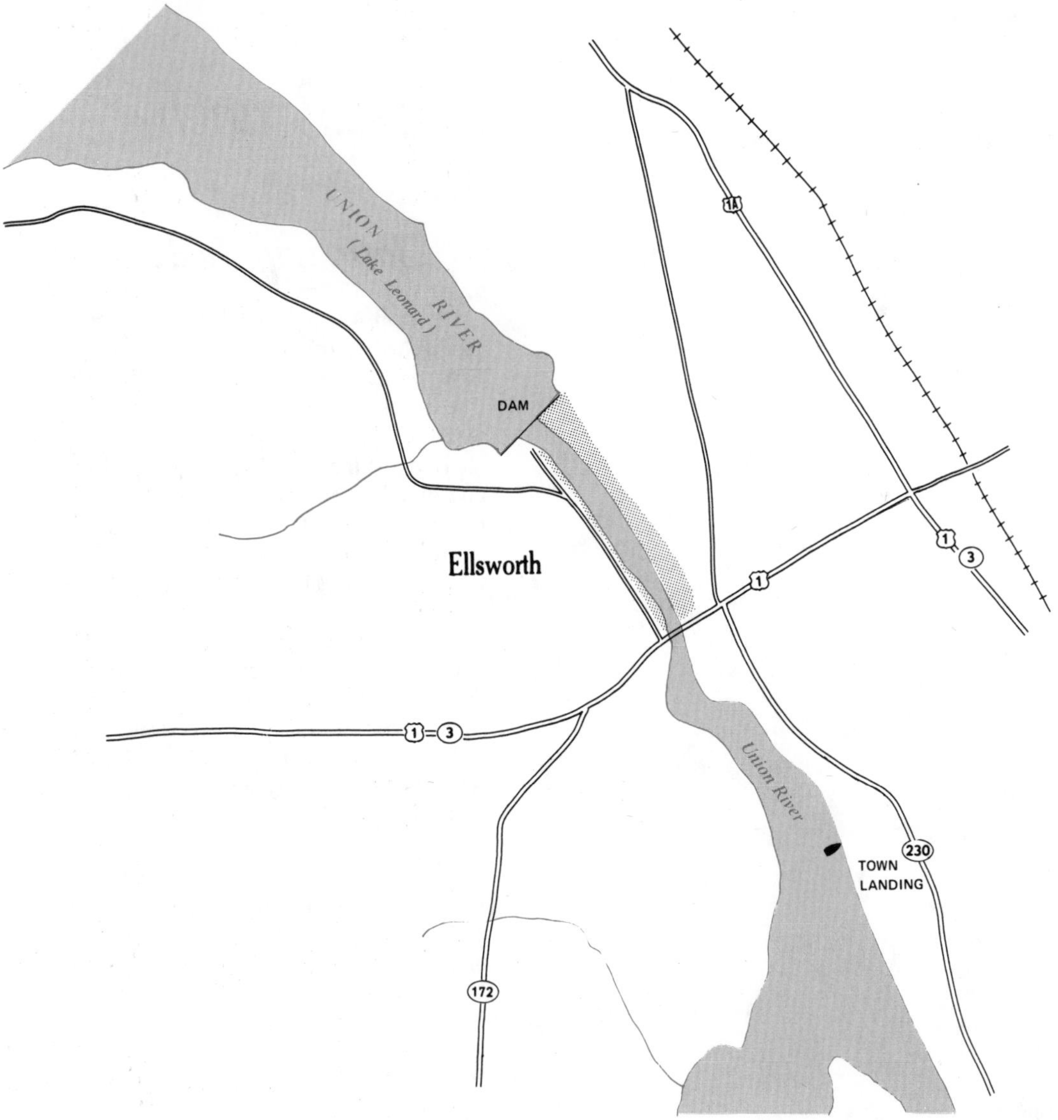

UNION RIVER (Lake Leonard)

DAM

Ellsworth

1A

1 3

1

1 3

Union River

230

TOWN LANDING

172

Union River

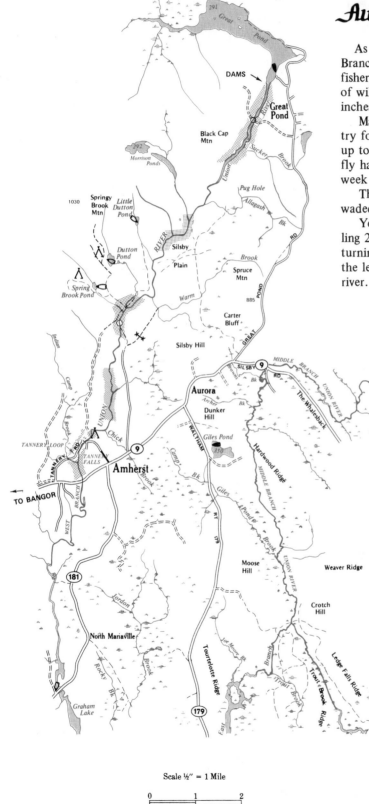

Scale ½" = 1 Mile

0   1   2

Miles

Middle Branch
Aurora

As is the case with the West Branch, the Middle Branch of the Union River has a good brown trout fishery based on stocked fish and also a population of wild brook trout. The brookies average 6 to 12 inches while the browns go from 10 to 14 inches.

May 1 to the end of June is the best season to try for the brook trout. The browns can be caught up to September 15. There are mayfly and caddis fly hatches from the third week of May to the first week of June.

There are sections of the river which can be waded and canoes can be put in at Route 9.

You can reach good fishing water by travelling 28 miles on Route 9 east out of Bangor and turning off onto Route 179. Watch for a road on the left just beyond Giles Pond which leads to the river.

West Branch
Great Pond
to Tannery Falls

A good brown trout fishery has been established in this section of the Union River which also has native brook trout. The brookies average 6 to 12 inches while the browns go from 10 to 14 inches.

Best fishing time is from May 1 to the end of June for brook trout. Brown trout can be taken up to September 15. There are mayfly and caddis hatches from the third week of May through the first week of June.

Wading conditions vary along the stream, but are generally difficult. Early in the season the stream can be canoed by putting in at Great Pond and taking out at Tannery Falls. The best fishing is in the two miles below Great Pond, at Silsby Plain (which requires a two-mile walk to reach), and in the Tannery Loop area.

This section of the river is located about 23 miles east of Bangor over Route 9. The countryside is rounded hills with a mixture of woods and fields.

Wassataquoik Stream
Baxter State Park to Penobscot River, East Branch

Penobscot and Piscataquis Counties
Maine Atlas map 51

Wassataquoik Stream is a true mountain stream and one of the prettiest places to fish in the state. This is not a place which could be canoed by any but the most intrepid whitewater fan.

Brook trout are the primary fish in the stream although there are a few landlocked salmon as well. The fishing is best in quiet places as the water rushes among the rocks and boulders. The fishing peak is from May 15 to June 15.

You can get to the upper reaches from Russell Pond Campground in Baxter State Park. The lower end would be reached by following Route 11 from Sherman to the Sherman Lumber Company Road.

Scale ½″ = 1 Mile

CANOEING DIRECTORY

A number of the rivers listed in this book are also popular canoeing streams, or are best fished from a canoe. The following directory gives brief descriptions of some of those canoe trips.

ALLAGASH RIVER - Telos Landing to Allagash Village, 98 mi: The longest wilderness waterway in Maine. Mixed whitewater, lakes and flatwater in beautiful hilly and forested setting. Many scenic attractions, 2 falls. Various possible trips, side trips; put-ins include Chamberlain Bridge (usual start), Allagash Lake, Churchill Dam, Umsaskis Bridge. (See DeLorme Allagash/St John map for complete guide information.)

AROOSTOOK RIVER - Several trips possible; mostly smooth fast water with occasional rips, through rural areas, settlements: Little Munsungan Lake to Oxbow; Oxbow to Ashland; Ashland to Fort Fairfield. Best at high water. Beginning of main river to Canadian border, 100 mi.

CARRABASSETT RIVER - Carrabassett to East New Portland, 23 mi: Continuous rapids and difficult pitches around boulders and ledges, runnable in medium but not high water (early May). Portage around dam. **East New Portland to North Anson, 8 mi:** Mostly smoothwater through meadows and woods.

COBBOSSEECONTEE STREAM - Cobbosseecontee Lake (outlet) to Rtes 126 and 9, 8 mi: Stream meandering through rolling countryside; 1 dam (portage), shallow spots at low water.

CROOKED RIVER - East Waterford to Scribners Mill, 17 mi: Flat, then several sets rapids (scout first). Meanders through forest, town, to several sets steep rapids, run by experts only (or portage). Then, mixed smooth and rapid, with 1 or 2 portages. **Scribners Mill to Edes Falls, 10 mi:** Mostly smooth and meandering, through woods and fields.

DEAD RIVER, NORTH BRANCH - Sarampus Falls to Eustis, 12 mi: Scenic stretch of smoothwater with strong current, some rapids and several difficult ledge drops (scout first).

DEAD RIVER, SOUTH BRANCH - Green Farm Bridge to Flagstaff Lake, 7 mi: Mostly quick and smoothwater through scenic woods, with several deep pools, some continuous and difficult rapids. Run before June.

DENNYS RIVER - Meddybemps to Dennysville, 17 mi: Mixed smooth and swift water, with several rips and short rapids. 3 dams, 1 steep drop; 4 portages.

EAST MACHIAS RIVER - Crawford Lake to East Machias, 33 mi: Mixed flat and rapid water through wild meadows, woods, across lakes. 1 dam, several short rapids. Run early in spring.

FISH RIVER - Round Pond to Portage, 20 mi: (Fly-in to lake, or private road access.) Smoothwater paddling through scenic wild country. Run at high water, no portages.

GRAND LAKE STREAM - Grand Lake Stream village to Big Lake, 3½ mi: Heavy rapids, 1 set of falls (portage); lesser rapids to lake.

KENDUSKEAG STREAM - Kenduskeag to Bangor, 16 mi: Fastwater with several sharp rapids and heavy drops, the second uncanoeable. Rapids lessen; flatwater to city. Best run at high water.

KENNEBEC RIVER, EAST OUTLET - Moosehead Lake to Indian Pond (NE end), 3½ mi: For experts only. Heavy and continuous rapids, narrow chutes, 1 sharp drop (portage). Fine run throughout season.

LITTLE OSSIPEE RIVER - North Shapleigh to Ossipee Mills, 11½ mi: Mixed flatwater, quickwater, rapids; high water recommended (run by end of April), or passage will be bony. Difficult rapids in Newfield not runnable; logs and beaver dams to portage. Attractive wooded area.

MACHIAS LAKES CIRCLE TRIP - Circle trip through Fourth Machias, Third Machias, Pocumcus, and Sysladobsis Lakes, 3-4 days: Chain of lakes linked by narrow, shallow streams; wilderness setting. Dam-controlled; run at moderately high water. 3 portages at dams.

MACHIAS RIVER - Big Machias Lake to Aroostook River, 32 mi: More or less continuous rapids, flowing among wooded mountains. Some difficult stretches; 2 portages around dams; deadwater section. Best earlier in summer.

MACHIAS RIVER - Third Machias Lake to Whitneyville, 51 mi: Highly scenic waterway in semi-wilderness area, comparable to Allagash. Includes whitewater, meandering streams, falls, lakes, ledge drops. Series of rapids, many runnable at high water (scout first); 5-8 portages. For experienced whitewater canoeists; guide recommended.

MATTAWAMKEAG RIVER, EAST BRANCH - Red Bridge to Haynesville, 20 mi: Mostly smooth paddling through woods, bogs. Some easy rapids, short carry at dam. Runnable throughout season.

MILLINOCKET STREAM - Millinocket Lake to Aroostook River, 6 mi: Fly-in recommended. Flatwater, easy rapids, except rough stretch to Millimagassett Stream. (Side trip up stream to very scenic lake.) Pretty country.

MOOSE RIVER - "Bow Trip," 34 mi: Cross Attean Lake, portage to Holeb Pond, circle back on Moose River. Mostly lake and flatwater paddling, with some rips and minor drops; several portages around falls, 1 long carry between ponds. One of the most popular canoe trips, beautiful mountain setting. Guide recommended. (To avoid long portage, start from Holeb Pond.)

NARRAGUAGUS RIVER - Deer Lake to Deblois, 23 mi: Mixed flatwater and rapids, meandering through scenic, hilly country, open meadows. 1 dam, drop. Sluggish at first, quickens to rips. Best at high water. **Deblois to Cherryfield, 15 mi:** Mixed fastwater, rapids (scout first) through barrens, wild valley. Portages around boulders, fall. Take out before town to avoid dams.

NESOWADNEHUNK STREAM - Nesowadnehunk Lake to Nesowadnehunk Field Campground, 4 mi: Easy rapids, pools, amid spectacular wilderness scenery. Runnable throughout season. (NOTE: Stream runnable to Daicey Pond Brook, but by experts only — numerous sharp drops.)

OSSIPEE RIVER - Kezar Falls to Cornish Station, 8 mi: Mostly quickwater through scenic woods and meadows; drops, series of rapids, split at rips (go left). 2-5 portages; best run in spring.

PENOBSCOT RIVER, EAST BRANCH - Matagamon Wilderness Campground to Grindstone, 38 mi: Mixed smooth, rapid, and fastwater, with series of impassable drops. 4-8 short portages around falls. Should be attempted by experienced canoeists; guide highly recommended. Run at medium high water. (NOTE: Contact Dudley's Matagamon Wilderness Campground for transportation arrangements.) Grindstone Falls and below, 1½-mi stretch of heavy rapids runnable by experts in favorable conditions only. **Below falls to Medway, 9 mi:** Mixed smoothwater and rips, one set difficult at high water.

PENOBSCOT RIVER, WEST BRANCH - Roll Dam (3 mi downstream from Seboomook Dam) to Ripogenus Dam, 45 mi: Mixed quick and flatwater paddling through scenic wilderness on winding river, big lake (windy). (Side trip to beautiful Lobster Lake.) 2½-mi portage around Rip Dam and gorge. (Contains very severe rapids, runnable by experienced team in whitewater raft.) **Big Eddy to Ambajejus Lake, 25 mi:** Mixed flatwater and rapids through forest, with several falls and stretches of heavy rapids, some dangerous, runnable only by experienced canoeists at low water. 3-7 portages, depending on water level and skill. (NOTE: From Rip Dam to Ambajejus Lake, recommended to go with whitewater rafting company expedition.)

ROACH RIVER - Kokadjo to Spencer Bay, 8 mi: Scenic rocky river. Some flatwater, mostly continuous rapids, some drops (runnable only at high water). Widens and slows toward lake.

ROYAL RIVER - Dunn's Corner to East Elm St, 10 mi: Easy flatwater paddling through pleasant rural area. Meandering; no obstructions. Runnable throughout season. (NOTE: In high water, trip can start as high as East Gray.)

SACO RIVER - Swans Falls to Great Falls, 33 mi: Mostly smooth, clear water meandering through pleasant rural and forested areas; only one short, easy stretch of whitewater (flooded out at high water). Take out upstream of log boom above falls. **Great Falls to East Limington, 20 mi:** Mostly flatwater through scenic countryside, with 5 sets of rapids, some difficult (at Steep Falls and Limington) and runnable by experts; 1-3 portages, depending on skill.

ST CROIX RIVER - Vanceboro to Kellyland, 33 mi: Mainly rapids, some difficult. For experienced canoeists; guide recommended. 3 portages at dams and falls. Water level regulated, runnable throughout season. **Kellyland to Calais, 20 mi:** Flatwater paddling to dam at Woodland, then mixed rapids, some heavy. 3 portages at falls, dam.

ST JOHN RIVER - Baker Lake (usual start) to Allagash Village, 110 mi: Challenging whitewater trip for experienced canoeists in remote wilderness setting. Several very heavy rapids. No portages, but guide recommended. Canoeable through mid-June; later, too shallow. Alternate put-ins include Fourth or Fifth St John Ponds (fly-in), Moody Bridge, Daaquam (Northwest Branch), Priestly Bridge, Dickey Bridge. (See DeLorme Allagash/St John map for complete guide information.)

SANDY RIVER - Smalls Falls to Phillips, 15 mi: Mixed continuous and severe rapids, some smoothwater. Runnable in medium water by experts, with 2 portages around gorges, 3-5 portages around steep drops. **Phillips to Farmington, 20 mi:** Quickwater, mixed rapids, boulders, some sharp drops requiring care. Smooth toward end.

SEBOEIS RIVER - Grand Lake Rd to East Branch Penobscot, 17 mi: Continuous, but not difficult, rapids through very scenic wooded valley. High water only recommended. Portage around falls.

SHEEPSCOT RIVER - North Whitefield to Wiscasset, 25 mi: Mostly smooth and meandering, with fastwater, 2-3 rapids, tidal effects. 1 portage. Take out at Head Tide, bridge at Sheepscot, or continue down estuary to Wiscasset. Best at high water; runnable into summer.

UNION RIVER, EAST BRANCH (STARVATION BRANCH) - Rte 9 to Rte 179 dam, 18 mi: Mixed smooth fastwater and easy rapids. 1 portage at dam. River runnable throughout season. (Trip could be extended to Graham Dam.)

BROOK TROUT STREAMS AND BROOKS

This list of streams and brooks known to contain brook trout was compiled from both experienced anglers and game warden sources.

In most cases the waters involved contain wild, self-sustaining populations of trout, although a few of these streams also contain stocked trout, particularly in Cumberland and York counties.

Most of the waters listed are small and correspondingly, so are the fish. In many of the smaller brooks listed, a six-inch brook trout would be a large fish, but other waters listed here may have fish of a pound or even more. Any brook or stream tends to be an extremely volatile habitat for trout, and the size and numbers of trout available are subject to extreme variations.

While this list does not include every stream in the state, it is good to keep in mind that in the northern two-thirds of the state almost any stream which does not dry up in the summer is likely to have a wild population of brook trout.

AROOSTOOK COUNTY

STREAM OR BROOK	TOWNSHIP	MAINE ATLAS MAP NUMBER AND GRID LOCATION	STREAM OR BROOK	TOWNSHIP	MAINE ATLAS MAP NUMBER AND GRID LOCATION
Armstrong Brook	T17 R4 WELS	Map 68, D-4	Little Black Stream	T18 R13 WELS	Map 70, C-5
Beaver Brook	T14 R5 WELS	Map 64, B-2	Little Madawaska River	Stockholm	Map 68, E-5
Big Brook	Littleton	Map 59, E-4	Little Musquacook		
B Stream	Houlton	Map 53, A-3	Stream	T12 R11 WELS	Map 62, D-3
Carry Brook	T16 R4 WELS	Map68, E-3	Mattawamkeag River,		
Chase Brook	T14 R9 WELS	Map 63, B-1	West Branch	Moro Plt.	Map 58, E-2
Chimenticook Stream	T17 R14 WELS	Map 70, E-5	Mill Brook	New Limerick	Map 53, A-2
Clark Brook	Westfield	Map 59, A-2	Mooseleuk Stream	T9 R8 WELS	Map 57, B-2
Cold Brook	Merrill	Map 52, A-4	Musquacook Stream	T13 R11 WELS	Map 62, C-2
Crystal Brook	Hersey	Map 52, B-1	North Pond Brook	T14 R8 WELS	Map 63, B-2
Dead Brook	Big Twenty Twp.	Map 66, A-2	Pattee Brook	Fort Fairfield	Map 65, C-4
Dickey Brook	T17 R5 WELS	Map 68, D-2	Pocwock Stream	T17 R13 WELS	Map 70, D-4
Dudley Brook	Merrill	Map 58, E-4	Pratt Lake Stream	T11 R9 WELS	Map 63, E-1
Dyer Brook	Island Falls	Map 52, B-3	River De Chute	Easton	Map 65, E-4
Fish Stream	Island Falls	Map 52, B-3	Rocky Brook	Mars Hill	Map 59, A-3
Five Finger Brook	T13 R11 WELS	Map 62, C-2	Rocky Brook	T19 R12 WELS	Map 66, B-1
Fling Brook	Easton	Map 65, E-3	Salmon Brook	Washburn	Map 64, C-4
Fox Brook, North Branch	T13 R9 WELS	Map 63, C-1	Salmon Brook, West		
Fox Brook, South Branch	T13 R9 WELS	Map 63, C-1	Branch	Perham	Map 64, B-4
Gardner Brook	Wade	Map 64, C-3	Sly Brook	New Canada Plt.	Map 67, D-5
Getchell Brook	Westfield	Map 59, E-2	Smith Brook	T14 R9 WELS	Map 63, B-1
Gizoquit Brook	Mars Hill	Map 59, A-4	Three Brooks	Blaine	Map 59, B-3
Glazier Brook	T11 R12 WELS	Map 62, E-1	Twentymile Brook	T12 R9 WELS	Map 63, D-1
Greenlaw Stream	T11 R7 WELS	Map 63, E-4	Wallagrass Stream	St. John Plt.	Map 67, D-2
Halfway Brook	Stockholm	Map 69, E-1	Whitney Brook	Bridgewater	Map 59, B-4
Hammond Brook	Cyr Plantation	Map 69, D-2	Whittaker Brook	T13 R13 WELS	Map 61, C-5
Hockenhull Brook	Fort Fairfield	Map 65, C-3	Wytopitlock Stream	Reed Plt.	Map 44, A-5
Lavoie Brook	Caswell Plt.	Map 69, E-4	Young Brook	Bridgewater	Map 59, B-3
Libby Brook	Mapleton	Map 64, D-4	Youngs Brook	Westfield	Map 59, A-2

CUMBERLAND COUNTY

Collyer Brook	Gray	Map 5, C-4	Muddy River	Naples	Map 4, B-4
Ditch Brook	Windham	Map 5, D-3	Northwest River	Sebago	Map 4, C-4
Eddy Brook	New Gloucester	Map 5, B-4	Piscataqua River	Falmouth	Map 5, D-4
Little River	Gorham	Map 5, E-2	Pleasant River	Windham	Map 5, D-3

FRANKLIN COUNTY

STREAM OR BROOK	TOWNSHIP	MAINE ATLAS MAP NUMBER AND GRID LOCATION
Barker Stream	New Vineyard	Map 20, B-1
Clear Brook	Chain of Ponds Twp.	Map 38, E-5
Fillibrown Brook	New Sharon	Map 20, D-3
Gilkey Brook	Freeman Twp.	Map 19, A-5
Goodrich Brook	New Sharon	Map 20, C-2
Hale Brook	New Sharon	Map 20, D-2
Hathan Bog Stream	Coburn Gore	Map 38, E-3
Horseshoe Stream	Massachusetts Gore	Map 38, E-4
Indian Stream	Chain of Ponds Twp.	Map 28, A-4
Lemon Stream	New Vineyard	Map 20, B-2
Massachusetts Bog Stream	Coburn Gore	Map 38, E-3

STREAM OR BROOK	TOWNSHIP	MAINE ATLAS MAP NUMBER AND GRID LOCATION
Mitchell Brook	Industry	Map 20, B-2
Moose River	Lowelltown Twp	Map 38, C-5
Muddy Brook	New Sharon	Map 20, C-2
Nash Stream	Coplin Plt.	Map 29, C-2
Orbeton Stream	Madrid	Map 29, E-2
Saddleback Stream	Sandy River Plt.	Map 19, A-1
Seven Mile Stream	Jay	Map 19, E-5
South Bog Stream	Rangeley Plt.	Map 28, E-4
Temple Stream	Avon	Map 19, B-4
Tim Brook	Tim Brook Twp.	Map 28, C-5
Webb River	Carthage	Map 19, D-2

HANCOCK COUNTY

Alligator Stream	T34 MD	Map 34, E-4
Bog River	Eastbrook	Map 24, C-4
Branch Lake Stream	Ellsworth	Map 24, E-1
Buffalo Stream	T39 MD	Map 34, C-2
Chick Brook	Amherst	Map 24, B-2
Chain Stream	T4 ND	Map 35, B-1
Colson Branch	T16 MD	Map 24, C-5
Coombs Brook	T41 MD	Map 34, D-5
Fifth Lake Stream	T41 MD	Map 35, D-1
Flanders Stream	Sullivan	Map 24, E-4
Frost Brook	Amherst	Map 24, B-1
Garland Brook	Mariaville	Map 24, C-1
Gassabias Stream	T41 MD	Map 34, D-5
Haynes Brook	Amherst	Map 24, B-2
Indian Camp Brook	Amherst	Map 24, A-2

Jellison Pond Brook	Mariaville	Map 24, B-2
Kilkenny Stream	Hancock	Map 24, E-2
Leighton Brook	Osborn	Map 24, B-3
Little Narraguagus River	T22 MD	Map 24, A-5
Mahanon Brook	T22 MD	Map 24, B-5
Marshall Brook	Southwest Harbor	Map 16, C-2
Meadow Brook	Orland	Map 23, E-3
Old Meadow Brook	Franklin	Map 24, D-3
Orland River	Orland	Map 23, E-3
Spring River	T16 MD	Map 24, C-5
Tannery Brook	Otis	Map 24, C-1
Twin Brooks	Amherst	Map 24, B-2
Warm Brook	Aurora	Map 24, A-3
Winkumpaugh Brook	Ellsworth	Map 23, D-4

KENNEBEC COUNTY

Bond Brook	Augusta	Map 12, C-5
Dearborn Brook	Windsor	Map 13, C-2
Great Meadow Stream	Rome	Map 20, E-4
Messalonskee Stream	Waterville	Map 21, E-1

Riggs Brook	Augusta	Map 13, B-1
Rome Trout Brook	Rome	Map 20, E-4
Sanford Brook	Belgrade	Map 12, B-4
Togus Stream	Chelsea	Map 13, D-1

KNOX COUNTY

STREAM OR BROOK	TOWNSHIP	MAINE ATLAS MAP NUMBER AND GRID LOCATION
Allen Brook	Appleton	Map 14, C-1
Fuller Brook	Warren	Map 14, E-1
Jam Brook	Searsmont	Map 14, C-2
Keene Brook	Rockland	Map 14, E-3

STREAM OR BROOK	TOWNSHIP	MAINE ATLAS MAP NUMBER AND GRID LOCATION
Little Medomak River	Washington	Map 13, C-5
Oyster River	Warren	Map 14, E-2
Pettengill Stream	Appleton	Map 14, C-1
Quiggle Brook	Union	Map 14, D-2

OXFORD COUNTY

STREAM OR BROOK	TOWNSHIP	MAP
Andrews Brook	West Paris	Map 11, B-1
Barker Brook	Bethel	Map 10, B-3
Bear River	Newry	Map 10, A-3
Bicknell Brook	Hebron	Map 11, D-3
Bog Brook	Hebron	Map 11, D-3
Bog Brook	Sumner	Map 11, B-2
Black Brook	Andover	Map 18, D-3
Cole Brook	Brownfield	Map 4, C-1
Dead Cambridge River	Upton	Map 17, C-5
Deer Mountain Stream	Adamstown	Map 28, E-2
Dragon Meadow Brook	Hiram	Map 4, C-3
Hobbs Brook	Stoneham	Map 10, C-2
Kedar Brook	Waterford	Map 10, D-4
Kendall Brook	Greenwood	Map 10, B-4
Langdon Brook	Stow	Map 10, E-1
Little Cold Brook	Stow	Map 10, E-1

STREAM OR BROOK	TOWNSHIP	MAP
Little Saco River	Brownfield	Map 4, B-2
Martin Brook	Lovell	Map 10, D-2
Mill Brook	Adamstown	Map 28, E-2
Nezinscot River, West Branch	Sumner	Map 11, B-2
Peabody Brook	Albany	Map 10, C-2
Pleasant River, East Branch	Albany	Map 10, C-2
Sawyer Brook	Andover	Map 18, D-3
Shepard River	Brownfield	Map 4, B-2
Sunday River	Newry	Map 10, A-3
Swift River	Roxbury	Map 18, C-5
Ten Mile River	Brownfield	Map 4, B-2
Twitchell Brook	Greenwood	Map 10, C-5
Wadsworth Brook	Hiram	Map 4, C-2
Wild River	Batchelders Grant	Map 10, B-1

PENOBSCOT COUNTY

STREAM OR BROOK	TOWNSHIP	MAP
Big Mud Brook	T2 R8 WELS	Map 51, E-2
Birch Stream	LaGrange	Map 33, C-1
Cold Stream	Greenfield	Map 34, D-1
Dead Stream	LaGrange	Map 33, C-1
East Ragged Brook	T4, Indian Purchase	Map 43, B-1
Ebhorse Stream	Chester	Map 44, D-1
Fish Stream	Patten	Map 52, C-1
Grant Brook	Long A Twp.	Map 43, B-2
Great Works Stream	Bradley	Map 23, A-5
Jerry Brook	TA R7 WELS	Map 51, B-4
Katahdin Brook	T3 R8 WELS	Map 51, D-3
Ledge Cut Brook	Millinocket	Map 43, B-3
Little Ebhorse Stream	Woodville	Map 44, C-1
Little Mud Brook	T2 R8 WELS	Map 51, E-2
Little Smith Brook	Millinocket	Map 43, B-3
Mattagodus Stream	Kingman	Map 44, C-4
Mattawamkeag River	Mattawamkeag	Map 44, C-2
Meadow Brook	Grindstone Twp.	Map 43, A-4
Meadow Brook	Soldiertown	Map 51, E-3

STREAM OR BROOK	TOWNSHIP	MAP
Mud Brook	Prentiss	Map 45, D-1
Nollesemic Stream	Hopkins Academy Grant	Map 43, B-3
Olamon Stream	Greenfield	Map 34, D-1
Partridge Brook	Long A Twp.	Map 43, B-2
Penobscot River, East Branch	Grindstone	Map 43, A-5
Pushaw Stream	Old Town	Map 33, E-3
Quakish Brook	T3 Indian Purchase	Map 43, B-2
Sally Ayres Brook	T2 R8 NWP	Map 43, D-4
Salmon Stream	Medway	Map 43, B-5
Sam Ayres Stream	T2 R9 NWP	Map 43, D-4
Sanborn Brook	TB R10 WELS	Map 42, C-4
Sandy Stream	T2 R8 WELS	Map 51, E-2
Schoodic Stream	Grindstone	Map 43, A-3
Seboeis River	T3 R7 WELS	Map 51, D-4
Smith Brook	T1 R8 WELS	Map 43, A-3
Soldier Brook	Soldiertown	Map 51, E-4
Sunkhaze Stream	Greenfield	Map 34, D-1

STREAM OR BROOK	TOWNSHIP	MAINE ATLAS MAP NUMBER AND GRID LOCATION
Swift Brook	Stacyville	Map 51, D-5
Swift Brook, East Branch	Stacyville	Map 51, D-5
Swift Brook, Middle Branch	Stacyville	Map 51, D-5
Swift Brook, West Branch	Stacyville	Map 51, D-5

STREAM OR BROOK	TOWNSHIP	MAINE ATLAS MAP NUMBER AND GRID LOCATION
Trapper Brook	Hopkins Academy Grant	Map 43, B-3
Trout Brook	Soldiertown	Map 51, E-3
Wadleigh Brook	T4 Indian Purchase	Map 43, A-1
West Ragged Brook	T4 Indian Purchase	Map 43, B-1

PISCATAQUIS COUNTY

STREAM OR BROOK	TOWNSHIP	MAP
Abol Stream	T2 R10 WELS	Map 50, D-4
Allagash Stream	T8 R14 WELS	Map 55, C-3
Bald Mountain Stream	Blanchard	Map 31, A-2
Big Wilson Stream	Greenville	Map 41, D-3
Blind Brook	T10 R9 WELS	Map 57, A-1
Cooper Brook	TA R10 WELS	Map 42, B-4
Cuxabexis Stream	T5 R12 WELS	Map 50, A-1
Dead Stream	Orneville	Map 33, B-1
Foss & Knowlton Stream	T2 R10 WELS	Map 50, D-5
Guernsey Brook	TB R11 WELS	Map 42, C-3
Katahdin Stream	T2 R10 WELS	Map 50, D-4
Little Nesowadnehunk Stream	T4 R10 WELS	Map 50, C-4
Lower Wilson Stream	Shirley	Map 41, E-2
Mooseleuk Stream	T9 R9 WELS	Map 57, B-1
Munsungan Stream	T8 R9 WELS	Map 57, C-1
Nahmakanta Stream	T1 R11 WELS	Map 42, A-3
Nesowadnehunk Stream	T4 R10 WELS	Map 50, C-4
Piscataquis River, East Branch	Shirley	Map 41, E-2
Piscataquis River, West Branch	Shirley	Map 41, E-2
Pleasant River, East Branch	TA R11 WELS	Map 42, B-3
Pleasant River, Middle Branch	Brownville	Map 32, A-4
Pleasant River, West Branch	Brownville	Map 42, E-4
Rainbow Stream	Rainbow Twp.	Map 50, E-3
Ripogenus Stream	T4 R12 WELS	Map 50, C-2
Russell Brook	Eagle Lake	Map 55, C-2
Sandy Stream	T4 R11 WELS	Map 50, C-3
Ship Pond Stream	Willimantic	Map 41, E-5
Smith Brook	T4 R11 WELS	Map 50, C-3
Snare Brook	T9 R13 WELS	Map 55, B-4
Soper Brook	T4 R11 WELS	Map 50, C-2
Thissell Brook	T5 R11 WELS	Map 50, A-3
Thoroughfare Brook	T9 R13 WELS	Map 55, B-4
Trout Brook	Nesourdnahunk Twp.	Map 50, B-4

WALDO COUNTY

STREAM OR BROOK	TOWNSHIP	MAP
Bartlett Stream	Montville	Map 14, A-1
Sheepscot River	Palermo	Map 13, B-5
Thompson Brook	Montville	Map 14, A-2

WASHINGTON COUNTY

STREAM OR BROOK	TOWNSHIP	MAP
Amazon Brook	Grand Lake Str. Plt.	Map 35, A-4
Barrows Stream	Crawford	Map 36, D-2
Beaverdam Stream	T26 ED BPP	Map 35, D-5
Big Springy Brook	T31 MD BPP	Map 35, E-4
Bog Brook	Cutler	Map 27, C-2
Bryant Brook	Northfield	Map 26, B-2
Chandler River	Centerville	Map 26, C-1
Crow Brook	Pembroke	Map 37, E-2
Deer Brook	T5 ND BPP	Map 35, B-2
Eastern Marsh Stream	Cutler	Map 27, C-1
Eastern Stream	Robbinston	Map 37, D-2
Freeman Brook	Steuben	Map 25, E-2

STREAM OR BROOK	TOWNSHIP	MAINE ATLAS MAP NUMBER AND GRID LOCATION	STREAM OR BROOK	TOWNSHIP	MAINE ATLAS MAP NUMBER AND GRID LOCATION
Grand Lake Brook	T6 ND BPP	Map 35, B-3	Oxbrook Brook	T6 ND	Map 35, A-3
Great Brook	Whitneyville	Map 26, B-2	Patten Pond Brook	Talmadge	Map 35, A-5
Great Marsh Stream	Columbia	Map 25, D-4	Pleasant River	Beddington	Map 25, A-1
Gould Meadow Brook	T27 ED BPP	Map 35, C-4	Pleasant River		
Harmon Brook	Crawford	Map 36, D-1	West Branch	Columbia	Map 25, D-4
Hobart Stream	Marion	Map 26, A-5	Pork Barrel Brook	T6 R1 NBPP	Map 35, A-3
Holmes Brook	T25 MD BPP	Map 25, B-5	Pottle Brook	Perry	Map 37, D-2
Holmes Stream	Whiting	Map 26, C-5	Rocky Lake Stream	Marion Twp.	Map 26, B-5
Indian River	Columbia Falls	Map 25, D-5	Scott Brook	Northfield	Map 26, B-2
Jim Brown Brook	Topsfield	Map 45, D-5	Seavey Brook	Wesley	Map 36, E-1
Kaylor Brook	Centerville	Map 25, C-5	Sipp Brook	Perry	Map 37, E-2
King Brook	T43 MD BPP	Map 35, C-3	South Brook	T27 ED BPP	Map 35, C-5
Lamsen Brook	Addison	Map 25, D-5	South Brook	T43 MD BPP	Map 35, C-3
Libby Brook	Centerville	Map 25, C-5	Southern Inlet	East Machias	Map 26, B-3
Little River	T43 MD BPP	Map 35, C-3	Tavern Brook	T43 MD	Map 35, C-3
Lively Brook	Whiting	Map 27, B-1	Taylor Brook	T18 MD	Map 25, A-4
Longfellow Brook	Whitneyville	Map 26, C-2	Tomah Stream	Forest	Map 45, C-5
Magurrewock Stream	Calais	Map 36, B-5	Trout Brook	Columbia	Map 25, D-4
Monroe Brook	T43 MD BPP	Map 35, C-4	Tunk Stream	Steuben	Map 25, E-2
Moosehorn Brook	Baring Plt.	Map 36, D-5	Wallamatogue Stream	T27 ED BPP	Map 35, C-5
Musquash Stream,			Wapasconhagan Brook	Alexander	Map 36, C-3
East Branch	Topsfield	Map 45, D-5	Western Stream	Robbinston	Map 37, D-2
Musquash Stream,			White Creek	Jonesboro	Map 26, D-1
West Branch	Talmadge	Map 35, A-4	Wiggins Brook	Trescott Twp.	Map 27, B-2
Ohio Brook	Pembroke	Map 37, E-1	Wilson Stream	Dennysville	Map 37, E-1

YORK COUNTY

STREAM OR BROOK	TOWNSHIP	MAINE ATLAS MAP NUMBER AND GRID LOCATION	STREAM OR BROOK	TOWNSHIP	MAINE ATLAS MAP NUMBER AND GRID LOCATION
Back Brook	Limington	Map 4, D-4	Lord's Brook	Lyman	Map 2, C-5
Bartlett Brook	Waterboro	Map 2, A-4	Mousam River,		
Branch Brook	Sanford	Map 2, D-4	Middle Branch	Alfred	Map 2, C-4
Buff Brook	Waterboro	Map 2, A-3	Muddy River	Naples	Map 4, B-4
Carlisle Brook	Lyman	Map 2, C-4	Northwest River	Sebago	Map 4, C-4
Chellis Brook	Parsonsfield	Map 4, E-1	Norton Brook	Shapleigh	Map 2, A-2
Chicks Brook	South Berwick	Map 2, E-4	Pease Brook	Cornish	Map 4, D-3
Davis Brook	Shapleigh	Map 2, A-2	Pendexter Brook	Parsonsfield	Map 4, E-2
Emerson Brook	Parsonsfield	Map 4, E-1	Pugsley Brook	Cornish	Map 4, D-3
Great Works River	South Berwick	Map 1, A-3	Pump Box Brook	Shapleigh	Map 2, B-2
Henderson Brook	Waterboro	Map 2, A-3	Shaker Brook	Alfred	Map 2, C-4
Junkins Brook	Hollis	Map 2, A-5	South River	Parsonsfield	Map 4, D-1
Kennebunk River	Lyman	Map 2, C-5	Stevens Brook	Wells	Map 2, E-5
Leavitt Brook	Limerick	Map 4, E-3	Sunken Brook	Lyman	Map 2, B-4
Little River	Cornish	Map 4, D-3	Wedgewood Brook	Parsonsfield	Map 4, E-1
Little River	Lebanon	Map 2, D-2			

BROWNS, BASS, SALMON AND PICKEREL
STREAMS AND BROOKS

This is a list of streams known to contain populations of brown trout, landlocked salmon, bass and pickerel.

Keep in mind while referring to this list that almost any stream feeding into or out of a lake, which is not blocked by a dam or fish screen, will at some time during the year contain whatever species of fish are found in the lake.

This is more true of brown trout and landlocked salmon than of bass or pickerel. Generally speaking, pickerel and bass will be found only in the slower and larger brooks and streams.

Abbreviations:

BN - Brown trout
BS - Bass
LS - Landlocked salmon
PK - Pickerel

CUMBERLAND COUNTY

STREAM OR BROOK	TOWNSHIP	MAINE ATLAS MAP NUMBER AND GRID LOCATION	STREAM OR BROOK	TOWNSHIP	MAINE ATLAS MAP NUMBER AND GRID LOCATION
Collyer Brook (BN)	Gray	Map 5, C-4	**Little River (BN)**	Gorham	Map 5, E-2
Ditch Brook (BN)	Windham	Map 5, D-3	**Piscataqua River (BN)**	Falmouth	Map 5, D-4

FRANKLIN COUNTY

STREAM OR BROOK	TOWNSHIP	MAP	STREAM OR BROOK	TOWNSHIP	MAP
Orbeton Stream (BN)	Redington	Map 29, E-2	**Webb River (BN, BS)**	Carthage	Map 19, D-2
Sevenmile Stream (BN, BS)	Jay	Map 19, E-5			

HANCOCK COUNTY

STREAM OR BROOK	TOWNSHIP	MAP	STREAM OR BROOK	TOWNSHIP	MAP
Alligator Stream (BN, LS)	Great Pond Plt.	Map 34, E-3	**Orland River (BN)**	Orland	Map 23, E-3
Branch Lake Stream (LS)	Ellsworth	Map 24, E-1	**Warm Brook (BN)**	Aurora	Map 24, A-3
Indian Camp Brook (BN)	Amherst	Map 24, A-2			

KENNEBEC COUNTY

STREAM OR BROOK	TOWNSHIP	MAP	STREAM OR BROOK	TOWNSHIP	MAP
Abagadasset River (BN)	Richmond	Map 12, E-4	**Hopkins Stream (PK, BS)**	West Mount Vernon	Map 12, A-3
Bond Brook (BN)	Augusta	Map 12, C-5	**Ingham Stream (PK, BS)**	Mount Vernon	Map 12, A-3
Great Meadow Stream (PK, BS)	Rome	Map 20, D-4	**Wilson Stream (BS)**	Monmouth	Map 12, C-2

KNOX COUNTY

STREAM OR BROOK	TOWNSHIP	MAINE ATLAS MAP NUMBER AND GRID LOCATION
St. George River (BN)	Appleton	Map 14, C-1

LINCOLN COUNTY

STREAM OR BROOK	TOWNSHIP	MAINE ATLAS MAP NUMBER AND GRID LOCATION	STREAM OR BROOK	TOWNSHIP	MAINE ATLAS MAP NUMBER AND GRID LOCATION
Eastern River (BN)	Whitefield	Map 13, D-1	Sheepscot River (BN)	Somerville	Map 13, C-4

OXFORD COUNTY

STREAM OR BROOK	TOWNSHIP	MAINE ATLAS MAP NUMBER AND GRID LOCATION	STREAM OR BROOK	TOWNSHIP	MAINE ATLAS MAP NUMBER AND GRID LOCATION
Magalloway River (LS)	Lynchtown	Map 27, C-5	Twitchell Brook (BN)	Greenwood	Map 10, C-5

PENOBSCOT COUNTY

STREAM OR BROOK	TOWNSHIP	MAINE ATLAS MAP NUMBER AND GRID LOCATION	STREAM OR BROOK	TOWNSHIP	MAINE ATLAS MAP NUMBER AND GRID LOCATION
Birch Stream (PK)	LaGrange	Map 33, C-1	Sandy Stream (S)	T2 R8 WELS	Map 51, D-2
Little Mud Brook (PK)	T2 R8 WELS	Map 51, E-2	Schoodic Stream (PK)	Grindstone	Map 43, A-3
Little Pattagumpus Stream (PK)	Woodville	Map 44, C-1	Seboeis River (BS)	T3 R7 WELS	Map 51, D-4
Parks Pond Brook (BS)	Clifton	Map 23, B-5	Wadleigh Brook (PK)	T4 IP	Map 43, A-1
Pushaw Stream (PK)	Old Town	Map 33, E-3			

PISCATAQUIS COUNTY

STREAM OR BROOK	TOWNSHIP	MAINE ATLAS MAP NUMBER AND GRID LOCATION	STREAM OR BROOK	TOWNSHIP	MAINE ATLAS MAP NUMBER AND GRID LOCATION
Big Wilson Stream (LS)	Greenville	Map 41, D-3	Rainbow Stream (LS)	Rainbow Twp.	Map 50, E-3
Nahmakanta Stream (LS)	T1 R11 WELS	Map 42, A-3	Ship Pond Stream (LS, BS)	Willimantic	Map 41, E-5
Pleasant River, West Branch (BS)	Brownville	Map 42, E-4	Togue Stream (LS)	T2 R9 WELS	Map 51, E-1

SAGADAHOC COUNTY

STREAM OR BROOK	TOWNSHIP	MAINE ATLAS MAP NUMBER AND GRID LOCATION	STREAM OR BROOK	TOWNSHIP	MAINE ATLAS MAP NUMBER AND GRID LOCATION
Cathance River (BN)	Topsham	Map 6, B-3			

SOMERSET COUNTY

STREAM OR BROOK	TOWNSHIP	MAP	STREAM OR BROOK	TOWNSHIP	MAP
Bog Stream (PK)	Mercer	Map 20, D-3	Sebasticook River (LS, BS, PK)	Harmony	Map 31, E-3
Carrabasseett Stream (BS, PK)	Canaan	Map 21, B-3	Wesserunsett Stream (BS)	Cornville	Map 21, A-1
Oak Stream (BS, PK)	Skowhegan	Map 21, B-2			

WALDO COUNTY

STREAM OR BROOK	TOWNSHIP	MAP
Sheepscot River (BN)	Palermo	Map 13, B-5

WASHINGTON COUNTY

STREAM OR BROOK	TOWNSHIP	MAP	STREAM OR BROOK	TOWNSHIP	MAP
Big Musquash Stream, East Branch (LS, BS, PK)	Talmadge	Map 35, A-5	Little Musquash Stream (BS, PK)	T43 MD BPP	Map 35, C-4
Big Musquash Stream, West Branch (LS, BS, PK)	Talmadge	Map 35, A-5	Little River (BS, PK)	T43 MD BPP	Map 35, C-3
			Little Wallamatogue Stream (BS)	T27 ED BPP	Map 35, C-5
			Wallamatogue Stream (BS)	T27 ED BPP	Map 35, C-5

YORK COUNTY

STREAM OR BROOK	TOWNSHIP	MAP	STREAM OR BROOK	TOWNSHIP	MAP
Davis Brook (BN)	Shapleigh	Map 2, B-2	Pendexter Brook (BN)	Parsonsfield	Map 4, E-2
Great Works River (BN)	South Berwick	Map 1, A-3	Salmon Falls River (BN)	Acton	Map 2, B-1
Kennebunk River (BN)	Arundel	Map 2, C-5	South River (BN)	Parsonsfield	Map 4, D-1
Littlefield River (PK)	Alfred	Map 2, C-4	Sunken Brook (BN)	Lyman	Map 2, B-4
Little River (BN)	Lebanon	Map 2, D-2	Ward Brook (BN)	Arundel	Map 3, C-1
Merriland River (BN)	Wells	Map 2, D-5			

HOW TO USE THE MAINE ATLAS AND GAZETTEER

On each map in this book, and in the additional listings at the back, are given Maine Atlas and Gazetteer map numbers and grid locations. These map numbers apply only to Seventh edition (1981) or later Atlases. The grid letters and numbers around the edges of each Atlas map will allow you to pinpoint the specific location of the river or stream in question. You can also go to the "Index of Maine Place Names" in the back of the Atlas and turn to the map number given for the town or township a river or stream runs through.